# Millionaire Baby

## Cracking the Wealth Code

## A Double Kaching Wedding

by

Suzanna N. Lam, CPA, MST

Bay Bridge Books
San Francisco, CA

ISBN: 978-0-9971086-6-8



Bay Bridge Brooks, Fremont, CA 94555
Printed in the United States of America.

First printing November 11, 2019.

"If you want 1 year of prosperity, grow grain.
If you want 10 years of prosperity, grow trees.
If you want 100 years of prosperity, grow people."

- *Chinese proverb*

# Millionaire Baby

## Cracking the Wealth Code

**A Double Kaching Wedding**

# Chapter One
## Matters of Betel and Areca

**"May you enjoy happiness for 100 years," said Arnie Vuong during a tea ceremony held in honor of his daughter, Emily, and her fiancée, David Nguyen.**

This was the kickoff event for what was going to be a very busy day.

It had already been busy.

Members of both families and a few close friends, about 30 people in all, had begun arriving at the Vuong family's San Jose home at eleven that morning.

The tea ceremony at the bride's home, a traditional part of celebrating a Vietnamese wedding, did not begin until noon. Afterwards, both families would make the 80-minute trip to the Nguyen family home in San Francisco for a second traditional tea ceremony. This second ceremony would be followed by a short drive to the Conservatory of Flowers in Golden Gate Park for a late-afternoon wedding and then a reception.

Arnie Vuong had not slept well the night before his daughter was to be married. He had been in and out of his bed half a dozen times throughout the night. But even when he lay in bed, he had not been able to close his eyes.

He had mostly been thinking about his daughter Emily and her fiancé, David. They had been dating a little over a year before they decided to get married. They had met while at Stanford; Emily had majored in Political

Science, and David had earned a degree in Mathematics. They were both 20 years old, both had graduated from college in three years, and both were enjoying the freedom that comes with being young. They were also getting ready to attend graduate school in Palo Alto in the Fall. Both David and Emily had been raised by parents who had fled the political turmoil in Vietnam in the 1970s, so both children had been raised to appreciate Vietnamese traditions as well as American ideals.

Arnie Vuong had smiled at the thought of how Emily and David had told him of their plans. They had invited him to dinner at Alexander's Steakhouse, a rather fancy restaurant west of downtown San Jose. Arnie had never been there before but was impressed with their choice the moment he arrived. The exterior was vaguely Japanese: a two-story building with a pagoda-style entryway complete with a slightly pitched roof, iron gates, and a stone walkway.

The restaurant was a bit pricey for recent college graduates, but Emily and David had insisted.

"Ahem, Mr. Vuong, you know Emily and I have been seeing each other for over a year now," David cleared his throat and began what seemed to Emily a decade long conversation

"Ah, yes, of course, I know, con," Arnie smiled. In Vietnamese culture when an elder speaks to a younger person, the term "con" means child is typically used.

"We get along very well and we uh, love each other very much." David's face started to turn red as Emily gently kicked his leg under the table.

Arnie stopped chewing his food and put on a more serious demeanor.

"Do you need some water, con? You don't look so well."

"Dad," Emily all of a sudden became more animated as she cut in, "David proposed to me last Sunday."

David shook his head, smiled sheepishly, and quickly drank his water to hide his embarrassment.

David, a good-looking young man with neatly-groomed black hair and a bright smile, suddenly grew serious, and Emily became quiet. A hopeful, expectant gleam was in her eyes. Arnie had not quite realized what was happening until David, with a degree of formality, which was rare even amongst those of Vietnamese descent, asked. "Mr. Vuong, may I marry Emily with your blessing?"

Before Arnie could say a word, Emily chimed in, "Don't worry, Dad, we consulted a fortune teller."

Arnie knew that his daughter was not a superstitious person and neither was David. They did not truly believe in the power of fortune tellers to predict anything; but they did believe in Vietnamese culture and Vietnamese traditions. Although he was not pleased that David didn't ask his parents to bring him the engagement news in the traditional Vietnamese way, he was pleased by the gesture of asking the advice of a fortune teller, which is seen as an acknowledgment to these traditions.

"What did the fortune teller say?" he asked.

"September 24th," Emily had said. "Three weeks before my 21st birthday."

"Well, congratulations! What are you two waiting for? Let's celebrate!" Emily and David looked at each other, nodded with pleasure, and then were quick to join Arnie in raising their Cabernet Sauvignon glasses in anticipation of their September wedding.

It would not be a traditional Vietnamese wedding, of course. It would be a fusion of Vietnamese and Western traditions. But a wedding was a wedding in any culture... or was it?

At four o'clock in the morning on September 24, 2011, Arnie Vuong finally gave up trying to sleep. He got up for good, showered and got dressed. He was alone in the house. His wife had passed away several years earlier. And his daughter had spent the last two days with friends in Norwood so he could decorate the house for the tea ceremony. He decided to go through the house one final time to make sure everything was ready. After he went through the house, he made himself a cup of Vietnamese coffee and sat down at the kitchen table. Once again he was soon lost in thought. But this time he was thinking about the life he had made for himself in America and the life he had left behind in Vietnam.

In America, he owned a beautiful split-level ranch in the Evergreen neighborhood of San Jose, California. It possessed all of the accoutrements one associated with an upper middle-class lifestyle. But its best feature, as far as Arnie was concerned, was a back-patio view of Mount Hamilton and the mountain range to the east of San Jose.

Arnie had bought the house because of the view. Whenever he looked at Mount Hamilton he thought about LangBiang Mountain in Dalat, Vietnam, a mountain he had visited on several occasions with his father as a boy. Of course LangBiang was more of a rural mountain, while Mount Hamilton rose above a landscape that was slowly being digested by urban sprawl, but both the mountain in his memory and the one he could see from his patio exerted a calming influence on his spirit.

Arnie also believed that his role as a father was defined in part by the very existence of mountains in general, and these two mountains in particular. On his very first visit to LangBiang Mountain, his father, a professor of Languages and Culture at The University of Saigon, had told him that the effort of a father is like a tall mountain, Công Cha Như Núi Thái Sơn. Arnie was only seven years old at the time and had not understood precisely what his father meant. His father had scooped him up and laughed at his confusion, but then he had assured his son that one day the meaning of his words would become clear.

Naturally, Arnie had hoped to become a professor like his father, but the Vietnam War had forced him to change directions on his journey into the future. Both of his parents had died during the war, so he stayed with an uncle. When Saigon fell, he immigrated with his uncle to the United States. He had earned a medical degree from UCLA in 1993 and now owned a pharmaceutical research company. He had succeeded in his life. In spite of the challenges that every refugee faces, he had made a very comfortable life for himself and his family in America. But it was only now, 44 years after that first visit to LangBiang, on the very day that his only child was about to embark on her own journey into the future, that he finally understood what his father had meant.

The first guest to arrive at the Vuong family home that day was Arnie's uncle. His Vietnamese name, which he never relinquished, was Buu Quang Vuong, but everyone called him Joseph, because he liked the Biblical story of Joseph's exile in Egypt.

"Am I the first one here?" Joseph burst out laughing.

"You are, Uncle. You know how it goes with Vietnamese time, rubberband time."

"Chúc mừng con, congratulations, nephew," Joseph extended his hand to shake Arnie's.

He followed Arnie into the house to a small sitting room that provided access to the patio through a sliding-glass door. The sitting room had been decorated for the tea ceremony in traditional Vietnamese fashion.

The main feature of the sitting room was an elegantly carved mahogany altar about the size of a buffet. The altar was covered with a red cloth with an orange-gold fringe. The cloth was decorated on the right side with a resplendent yellow, green and blue Phoenix, a mythic bird with a long tail that represented the bride. On the left side, facing the Phoenix, was a gold and green Dragon that represented the groom. Directly above the Phoenix and the Dragon were the words *Trăm năm hạnh phúc,* a Vietnamese phrase that means "100 Years of Happiness."

On the wall directly behind the altar was a red cloth banner with the same images, the same phrase as the altar covering.

An ornately decorated incense burner occupied the center of the altar with a brass candlestick on either side, each with a red candle. On the right side of the altar there was a bowl of fruit and a bottle of wine. On the left side there was a flower vase dripping with red orchids.

"Now, let's get the fireworks ready!" said Arnie.

Joseph was smiling a broad smile as they headed out to the patio.

At precisely eleven o'clock, a long black limousine pulled up to the curb outside Arnie Vuong's home. Several more black limos pulled in behind the first one. The car doors opened all at once, almost as if the entire sequence had been rehearsed. David Nguyen, emerged from the first vehicle after Abby, and Daniel. David's aunties and uncles also emerged from other vehicles with elaborated red trays of fruits, baked goods, flowers, batel leaves, and a large barbecued baby pig wrapped nicely in special glossy and see-through red gift wrap. They were beaming at each other and started up the brick walkway towards the house.

David, who was wearing a traditional blue silk suit (also called an *ao dai*) embroidered with dozens of golden suns and a blue silk turban hat, stepped into the house with much anticipation.

Emily was dressed in a traditional long red dress, an *ao dai,* made of silk and embroidered with dozens of golden Phoenixes. She was also wearing a *khan dong,* a red silk hat that wrapped around her head (almost like a turban), and holding a bouquet of white roses in her left hand. She was waiting inside her bedroom.

An entourage filled in behind the groom. Two young men, also in blue silk suits but without the fancy embroidery, walked directly behind David. The men were each holding a red oversized umbrella decorated with Vietnamese symbols. Four young women in yellow silk *ao dais*, each holding a bouquet of purple heliotrope, followed the umbrellas. Finally, various members of the groom's family and other guests followed the official wedding party. The men were wearing black suits, Western style tailored suits. The women were wearing designer *ao dais* by Calvin Hiep. Some were carrying gifts, a few red trays like the one Joseph had brought, a few red lacquered boxes, elaborately carved and covered with red cloth.

The wedding party did not enter Arnie Vuong's house through the front door. As they approached the house they passed through a gated archway and found themselves in a rather expansive patio area that featured slate-gray patio tile and wrought iron patio furniture. The patio wrapped around the side and back of the Vuong family house. Along the eaves of the house, Arnie had hung a series of paper lanterns of various colors. In the distance they could see the mountains to the east. The view was majestic.

The moment they entered the patio area, there was a burst of fireworks to ward off evil spirits and welcome the groom and his family.

The tea ceremony began in front of the altar. Arnie lit the incense burner and the spicy sweet aroma of incense filled the room. He said a short prayer, asking his ancestors to bless the marriage between Emily and David. Mostly he was praying to his wife. Then he lit the candles and stepped back from the altar. Then each elder of Emily's family took turn speaking and giving the couple red envelops which contained sizable amount of cash inside. In Vietnamese tradition, when the groom's family visits the bride's family on the wedding day, the bride's side of the family would give her sage advice about love, marriage as though to show the groom's family "look, you see how we teach our girl? so if she turns out not to be the person that you thought she was it's not our fault. "

When all her great uncles, great aunts, uncles, aunts on both side of her family were done with their good wishes and advice, then Emily thanked her parents for the sacrifices they had made on her behalf. Emily and David bowed to Arnie. They bowed to each other. Then they began serving tea to the guests.

To Arnie, the next hour was a blur. All he could think about was his wife and how much he missed her. From the day Emily had been born, all his wife could talk about was the joy of having a daughter and how that joy would be multiplied on the day that Emily got married. But she had died eight years earlier of breast cancer. He had never even heard of breast cancer before coming to America. But after his wife had died from the disease, he decided then and there that he was going to do what he could to find a cure. That's when he had founded his pharmaceutical research company. He and his wife had been denied the 100 years of happiness they had dreamed about on the day of their wedding. They had been granted the blessing of their daughter, but they had been denied the joy of each other's company. He was determined that others would not suffer the same fate. His company's name was Hanh Phúc Pharmaceuticals, in memory of his wife.

"Hello dear father of the bride. I would like you to meet my grandmother."

For a moment Arnie could not tell where he was or who was talking. He turned to the sound of the voice as a sleepwalker turns.

"She is sitting out on the patio telling stories."

Arnie smiled. The voice belonged to Abby Nguyen, David's mother.

Arnie and Abby had first met one month earlier for lunch at a restaurant in downtown San Francisco called The Slanted Door. They had met to discuss some of the details of the wedding between their children, but the conversation had encompassed a variety of subjects, from their past lives in Vietnam to the hardships brought on by the war, to life in America, to the trials they as refugees had endured on their way to achieving success.

Abby was a successful real estate developer and had a reputation for making good financial decisions. She was also very direct.

"Yes, but what provisions have you made to pass on your wealth to your daughter?" Abby had asked. "What are you doing to preserve your legacy? What are you going to do to help her and her new family?"

Of course. He had to admit that he had done next to nothing about his legacy. The only reason he even had a will was because of his wife. He had been too focused on work, on making his company a success. He made very good money now, but it went out almost as quickly as it came in. When Abby found out that he was going to pay for his daughter's wedding expenses out of his own pocket, she quickly launched into an explanation of the value of IULs (Indexed Universal Life Insurance).

It was the first time Arnie had ever heard the term.

"So you mean you're borrowing from yourself to pay for David's wedding expenses and you're earning money at the same time?" Arnie was somewhat incredulous.

"Exactly!" said Abby. "That's the beauty of an IUL. Instead of paying the interest on the loan to a bank, you pay the interest to yourself. You are the bank!"

"It sounds too good to be true," said Arnie. "I want to know more."

The following week he had met with Michiko in her downtown San Francisco office. Two days later, he had purchased an IUL for himself and another one for Emily. It was going to be a wedding present. And as soon as Emily and David started having kids, he was going to buy IULs for each of them, no matter how many children they decided to have.

"*Bà Ngoai,*" said Abby. "This is Mr. Vuong, Emily's father." *Bà Ngoai* was the Vietnamese word for one's maternal grandmother. For Abby, it was also a term of endearment.

"Ah, Mr. Vuong, your daughter and my great-grandson make a beautiful couple, do they not?"

"Yes, Ms. Trần, they do," Arnie said.

"It has been many years since a warm Spring breeze has melted the ice on our doorstep," said Ms. Trần. "But now Spring has returned."

Arnie looked confused and Abby laughed at his confusion.

"My grandmother has a fierce warrior spirit coupled with a poet's heart," Abby said.

"Do sit down, Mr. Vuong," said Ms. Trần.

"Yes," said Abby. "I will return shortly."

Abby Nguyen's maternal grandmother had originally immigrated to Vietnam from Hainan Island, China in 1937. Her Chinese name was Chen Lei. But in 1954, the year that Vietnam was split into two separate countries because of the failure of the politicians at the Geneva Convention, the government of South Vietnam took steps to quicken the pace at which Chinese-born citizens were assimilated into Vietnamese society. In 1956, the government passed a law requiring those born in China to swap their Chinese names for Vietnamese ones. So Chen Lei became Trần Le, or Ms. Trần for short.

Arnie pulled up a wrought-iron chair and sat down opposite Ms. Trần. She was a small, wiry woman, thin bony arms and fingers, but she carried herself with the grace of a dancer. She had a few cracked and crooked teeth but she smiled anyway. She always seemed to be smiling. She was wearing a white wool knit cap in spite of the fact that it was 72 degrees.

There were five other people crowded around the small circular table, all of them young people, friends of David and Emily. All of them were listening with curious attention to everything Ms. Trần said.

For a while Ms. Trần talked about her life as a young girl on Hainan Island and how she and her family had escaped in 1936 because the Japanese were invading China.

Then she talked about her life in Vietnam until the fall of Saigon in 1975.

Then she looked Arnie squarely in the eye and began to tell a story, a mythic story from Vietnam. Arnie was certain the story contained a hidden message, a bit of ancient wisdom that he had once known, but had forgotten, so he listened carefully.

*"Once upon a time, there lived a poor woodcutter and his family in a small bamboo hut near the banks of a wide river. The woodcutter barely made enough money from the wood he cut to feed his family, but he was diligent and worked hard every day, so his family never went hungry. Then one day, while he was hard at work cutting down trees that had taken root along the river bank, his ax suddenly and mysteriously slipped from his hand and flew into the middle of the river. It sank to the bottom before he could utter a single word.*

*"Now, it so happened that this particular river was inhabited by a magical river dragon. The river dragon approached the poor woodcutter, who was still staring in blank-faced amazement at the spot where his ax had disappeared. 'What is the matter, woodcutter?' said the river dragon. 'Why have you stopped chopping down trees?'*

*"'It is my ax,' said the poor woodcutter. I was swinging it as I always do, and then it just slipped from my fingers. Now I do not know what will happen. I will have to find another ax. Without an ax my family will surely starve."*

*"The river dragon smiled an inscrutable smile and said 'Perhaps I can help.' And with that he swam out to the middle of the river and dove to the bottom. A moment later he returned with a beautiful golden ax, the likes of which the poor woodcutter had never seen, not even in his dreams. 'Here is your ax, woodcutter,' the river dragon said.*

*"But the poor woodcutter, who could not take his eyes off the beauty of the golden ax, said 'No, this is not my ax. My ax has a handle made of hickory and a blade made of iron.'*

*"So the river dragon swam out to the middle of the river a second time and dove to the bottom and moments later returned with a second ax made of the finest silver, the likes of which the poor woodcutter had only ever heard about when he and his friends would gather around a small fire after dark to talk and drink and tell tall tales. 'Here is your ax, woodcutter,' the river dragon said.*

*"But the poor woodcutter, who was remembering some of the tall tales he used to tell, said 'No, this is not my ax. My ax has a handle made of hickory and a blade made of iron.'*

*"So the river dragon swam out to the middle of the river and dove to the bottom a third and final time and returned moments later with an ax that had a handle made of hickory and a blade made of iron. 'Here is your ax, woodcutter.'*

*"The poor woodcutter was overjoyed and asked what he could do to repay the river dragon for the gift of retrieving his ax. But the river dragon only smiled his inscrutable smile and said 'No, no, you are an honest man, and honesty should ever be rewarded, so in addition to*

*retrieving your iron ax, I am giving you the silver ax and the golden ax to do with as you wish.'*

*"Then the river dragon vanished, and the poor woodcutter realized he was no longer so poor. But he also realized that his good fortune was not just the result of his honesty. Heaven had blessed him because he had a good heart, and because he was willing to work hard to feed his family no matter what circumstances he encountered."*

It was at that point, as the story concluded, that Abby returned.

"It's time to head back to San Francisco," she said to her grandmother. "We have another tea ceremony, and then a wedding, and then the reception."

The five friends of Emily and David vanished in a flash, but Abby and her grandmother took their time getting up from the table.

"Your grandmother is quite a storyteller," Arnie said. "I thoroughly enjoyed listening to her."

"Yes," said Abby. "I spent many, many hours listening to her when I was growing up. So did David. Isn't that so, *Bà Ngoai*?"

"There is not much else to do but tell stories when one reaches my age," said Ms. Trần, and she laughed softly.

"She is the reason I am a success," said Abby

The two women made their way across the patio, talking in low murmurs, measuring each step. But before they passed through the arched gateway, Abby turned and looked at Arnie with joyful eyes.

"Welcome to the family," she said.

# Chapter Two
## Wedding of the Ages

**"That went very, very well, don't you think, hon? Seems like it went off without a hitch. You, Emily and David did a fantastic job of planning."**

As Abby and Daniel walked to their car, arm in arm, Daniel was quick to remark about the day's festivities.

"Yes, it did go well, didn't it?" replied Abby, with a smile of satisfaction. "It was a beautiful ceremony. All of our guests seemed to enjoy themselves and David seemed so happy."

"I agree, hon. We can only hope that David and Emily enjoy the same happiness that you and I have had. I never could have imagined I could be this happy," mused Daniel.

"Seems like our love continues to grow, even after all these years. You've made me a very happy man, Abby."

"And if you are ever looking for another career, it seems you've found a calling as a wedding planner," teased Daniel. "You and Jennifer Lopez. Birds of a feather flock together."

Daniel couldn't help but laugh at his own joke.

Abby smiled at Daniel as he opened the passenger door of their Tesla and ushered her inside before closing the door.

Abby knew full well that Daniel had been aware of

the trials and travails she had with her mother Ms. Kim and with her future daughter-in-law Emily in planning the special day for their son David. Although Daniel had been mostly on the sidelines during these disagreements, he had always offered a kind ear to Abby as she vented her frustrations regarding the differing opinions of Ms. Kim and Emily.

Ms. Kim was of the belief that David and Emily's wedding offered her family an opportunity to display their wealth and standing. Since arriving as an immigrant from Vietnam, Ms. Kim had worked hard to create success and a place for herself in the new country. She had started doing manicures and pedicures in a nail salon and had parlayed her hard work and acquired expertise into owning her own salon. With Abby's help, Ms. Kim had expanded her financial success into a chain of franchised nail salons. That success had been profiled in a national franchise magazine. The article even labeled Ms. Kim as *The Empress of Nails*. Ms. Kim reluctantly accepted that new title from her family members, who were quick to tease her about that.

Ms. Kim was so proud of the fame and fortune she had achieved since coming to America. And Abby was always quick to laud her mother's hard work and subsequent success.

When Ms. Kim found out that her only grandson was getting married, she quickly made it known to Abby that she thought David's wedding should be a "wedding for the ages." She opined that there should be no budgetary limitations for the special once-in-a-lifetime celebration of her grandson and his bride-to-be.

Ms. Kim told Abby that the costs of the wedding should not be a consideration and that there should be no regard for the number of guests invited.

"The more, the merrier. Is that how they say it?"

"Well, mother, that is not for you to decide," Abby had cautioned Ms. Kim. "That is up to David and Emily."

"Well, daughter, please tell all involved that I am happy to pay all expenses. Our family has accumulated considerable wealth over the years, and I want my grandson to know that we will spare no expense on this special day of his."

Abby already knew that her son, David, and she shared fiscal conservatism. As a recent Stanford grad, David was bound and determined to create his own success and his own wealth. David was a bright young man who had earned a partial scholarship to Stanford. Abby and Daniel fronted the additional funds necessary for tuition and living expenses. Unlike some people his age, David had frequently expressed his gratitude to his parents for their financial contributions. And he was always quick to remind them that he would be sure to make them proud with whatever he did with his life.

"Well, the days of your father and I being your ATM machine will finally end after you graduate," Abby had smiled as she teased her son. "You'll be on your own soon."

Abby already knew David's hopes and dreams for creating his own financial nest and treasure trove. David had apparently inherited some of Abby's interests and ambitions. He and some of his college buddies were already working to scrounge enough money together to invest in some modest rental properties. At Stanford, he'd been part of a very successful investment club, which had taught him the peaks and pitfalls of the stock market and made him some extra spending money. David had told Abby and Daniel that when he finished college, he was anxious to accumulate enough wealth to purchase a starter home for he and Emily. Abby was proud to see that David had absorbed some of her financial acumen.

She was sure that he'd be financially successful in providing for Emily and their future kids.

Emily, however, was an entirely different story, as Abby had learned as the wedding neared. Emily was bright, respectful, and personable. However, as an only child, she'd always been given everything she asked for. Her father, Arnie, the owner of a pharmaceutical research company, had done very well for himself and his family.

When Arnie first met his future in-law Abby, he admitted to Abby that he was good at making money, but he wasn't good at investing or tracking the money he made. And it seemed that Emily had inherited some of her father's financial indifference. Arnie had even joked, "I love my daughter, Abby, but I'll admit that I'll be glad to let David see if he can get through to her regarding finances. I've never been successful in doing that. Seems she always been my pampered princess."

Abby had almost choked on her garlic bread when she's heard Arnie talking about the spending habits of her future daughter-in-law. Thankfully, she was able to let Arnie's observations pass and they enjoyed the rest of their dinner. But Arnie's pampered princess label for Emily stuck with Abby and, in planning for the wedding, she soon realized that Arnie's assessment of his daughter had been accurate.

At dinner at the Boulevard one night soon after, Emily had told Abby and Ms. Kim of her dreams for an ostentatious wedding. (Ostentatious was Abby's word, not Emily's.) David had remained very quiet throughout the discussion, occasionally rolling his eyes to his mother when Emily wasn't looking. Abby was surprised to see that her son was yielding to Emily regarding matters of the wedding, when he had been so adamant about a sensible wedding in conversations with Abby.

Abby wondered if Emily was already wearing the

pants in the family. Or had David had this same conversation with Emily many times before without success and was now going to simply sit back and observe how his mother would handle it?

"Emily, dear, I'm interested in what you have to say about the money you'd be spending on a large wedding instead of a moderate wedding," Abby hesitantly broke the ice and continued. "Daniel and I have talked about giving the two of you some seed money toward a down payment on a starter home, as your wedding present. Are you telling me that you would rather use that money for a larger wedding? We've already told you what we are willing to give you some money toward your wedding, but that's not nearly enough to cover the type of wedding you're talking about now."

"Well, my wedding day will be the biggest day of my life, Abby. I've dreamed of having a big wedding ever since I was a little girl. I want everything to be special, everything to be perfect. I want people to see how happy David and I are."

"Of course, dear, I want the two of you to have a lovely wedding," Abby assured Emily. "But the wedding you're describing now is approaching $150,000. I hate to see you spend all that money for just one day. Memories are important, but they should be balanced with practicality, don't you think? Daniel and I got married on a shoestring budget, and, even to this day, the people who know us know how happy we are together."

Emily quickly glanced at David with a smile, and then slightly tilted her head on his right shoulder, while squeezing softly on his thigh under the table.

"Well, Abby, David and I appreciate any funds you and Daniel can give us to finance the wedding. Whatever you can't cover, David and I will pick up ourselves. Or maybe we can get my father to pitch it."

"The two of you just graduated from college," Abby

reminded them of the obvious. "Where do you plan to get the money to cover a large wedding?"

"Well, maybe we can take out a loan. Could we do that, David?"

David, who had slowly been turning purple as the conversation progressed, finally broke his self-imposed silence. "I'm not sure that's a good idea, Emily. We don't really have any collateral to offer and I'm not sure a bank is going to consider a wedding a sound investment."

"Maybe we can get a loan from my father."

"Oh, my dear child, don't you worry about having enough money for the wedding, I'll pay for it all"

All three heads turned all at once in the direction of what was just being said. Ms. Kim, sitting comfortably in her chair fixing her reading glasses didn't even look up. She seemed to be occupied with the dessert menu contemplating whether she should have a classic French Napoleon or a strawberry Napoleon.

"Oh, Mom, are you done picking your dessert? I think they're closing soon and we have to get going," Abby found a way to divert the non-invited comment hoping no one really paid attention to Ms. Kim

"Of course, I'll have a strawberry Napoleon but in all fairness to Emily I'd like to pay for the entire wedding including their honeymoon considering Emily is the only grand-daughter in law and David is my only grandson."

A heavy cloud of silence descended and stayed there for what seemed to be a dial up internet connection until the waiter came back with Ms. Kim's dessert.

"How about we talk about this later?" said David, pulling out his credit card and motioning for the waiter.

"Let me get this, you two," said Abby, pushing David's credit card away. "Why don't the two of you discuss the things we talked about tonight and then let's talk again this weekend. These are some big decisions to make and we shouldn't make them all tonight," Abby hoped Emily would become more practical as she thought about what Abby had said.

"We're all set, the tab had been paid," the waiter signaled the party of four.

Ms. Kim slyly smiled and winked to the disappointment of Abby and David.

As they quietly left the Boulevard, David felt disappointed to have his mother, his grandma involved in the first major disagreement of his relationship with Emily. He hoped that his mother's advice for Emily would take root. He was also glad that his grandma had volunteered to pay for the entire wedding which would mean Emily and he wouldn't have to worry about any cost of the wedding. All of the sudden, he caught himself being torn by his Mom's financial discipline and his grandma's generosity. He'd previously expressed similar sentiments in discussions with his bride-to-be, but without any signs of success. He loved Emily, but trying to get her to waver on her thoughts of an extravagant wedding was like talking to a wall. Now, with the support of his grandma, it seems Emily was winning the argument once again. He didn't want is mother to be on the lighter side of the scale still. He wished Emily and he didn't have a wedding.

# Chapter Three
## The Tail of the Dragon

**"Remember my father once took me to see a play put on by street performers," said Ms. Trần.**

Abby could not help but smile as she approached her grandmother, who was sitting in an easy chair in the living room of Abby's condo in the Opera Plaza building on Van Ness Avenue in San Francisco.

The second tea ceremony had ended thirty minutes earlier, but the wedding wouldn't start for another hour-and-a-half. Abby had known the day was going to be hectic, so she had purposefully built in a little down time so everyone could catch their breath.

Her grandmother was holding court, so to speak, in the living room. In fact, every chair in the living room was occupied, as was the sofa. And no one was admiring the view of the bay, which was glistening in the distance. Instead, everyone was listening to Abby's grandmother tell stories.

"Please forgive my interruption, everyone," said Abby. "But we will be leaving for the wedding in 30 minutes. I just wanted you to know. Is there anything I can get anyone?"

There was a chorus of "no thanks, Abby" and a few people shook their heads and smiled politely.

"Then I'll let you get back to my grandmother's tall tales," Abby smiled. "Remember *Bà Ngoai*, we have to leave in 30 minutes."

"Do not worry granddaughter," said Ms. Trần. "I will not let the present be hijacked by the past."

Abby smiled and headed into the kitchen. Her grandmother loved an audience. And audiences loved her grandmother.

"My father had never taken me to see a street opera before," said Ms. Trần. The voice of Abby's grandmother echoed throughout the condo. For some reason, whenever she started talking about her past, she always began with the story of the day her father took her to see a street play, what the Chinese called Qiong Opera, in the town of Wenchang on Hainan Island, China, some 50 miles southeast of the Island's capital, Hoihow. Her grandmother had been born in Wenchang in 1923. She often said that at that time Wenchang had been a thriving community of merchants and artisans.

"But on my sixth birthday," said Ms. Trần, "my father said I was old enough, so off we went. This was in 1929, four years after General Sun Yat-sen had died, though I did not know this at the age of six. But I tell you this now so you will understand the chaos that existed in Wenchang in those days. The General had been the first President of the Republic of China in 1912, but his government had collapsed a year later. The whole of China was embroiled in political turmoil for the next 20 years, but the sense of lawlessness was more pronounced on Hainan Island than anywhere else in the country. Soldiers patrolled the streets of every city, civil district and town on the island, but this did not put anyone at ease because the soldiers were often the ones who ransacked local businesses, taking whatever they wanted. Everyone was afraid of stray bullets. It was the same in 1929 as it had been when General Sun had died, and even before, when the General had been forced to leave China for a time.

"So the day my father took me to see the street

performers, the streets were filled with soldiers roaming the streets. Mostly they were bothering students, because the students were always protesting, gathering in large groups and causing almost as many problems as the soldiers for everyday people. But there was a lot of unrest in those days. Every day, thousands of people were buying passage aboard a steamer in the harbor at Hoihow to take them to Penang or Singapore or Kuala Lumpar. Somewhere away from China. And everyone who stayed on Hainan Island was dissatisfied with one thing or another. The textile workers were always going on strike, or some other industry, and the police were always called in to break up any demonstrations. Everywhere people were making speeches against the Japanese and calling for a boycott of anything made in Japan because the Japanese had flooded China with their yen. There was violence in the rural villages, which caused a series of food shortages. And the Communists, who had been expelled from the mainland, were on every street corner, preaching their gospel of revolution. It was a crazy situation. Even the religious were not safe. The year before General Sun died, a missionary was attacked and killed by bandits on the road from Kacheck to Hoihow. But this is the way it was."

"Weren't you frightened?" said a voice from the sofa.

"I was not frightened," said Ms. Trần. "But as I said, I did not know about any of the politics and the turmoil when I was six. To me the streets were filled with exotic sights and sounds and glorious smells. I remember we were walking along Wennan Street, which was filled with vendor's stalls and merchants standing in front of their shops along the arcade, waving at my father to come inside and purchase a small gift for his daughter, a candle perhaps, or some other small item. And I wanted to go inside and see what they were selling, but my father only laughed and waved back.

"'We must hurry my little Lei,' my father said. "The performance will begin shortly.'

"So we hurried down the street, and soon we came to a large open area where Wennan and two other streets came together. The street performers had set up their stage in this open area. It was a big wooden, platform stage with four heavy, wooden posts, one on each corner, to hold up a canvas roof. The roof was for the actors, not the audience. The audience stood milling about in the street. It was so crowded I could not see, so my father hoisted me onto his shoulders and I grabbed hold of his hair so I would not fall by accident.

"When the performers began, I thought I had entered a dream. I am not sure what the story was about. I remember there was a king with a big black beard and he was shouting at two soldiers to take care of something. Then he beat one of the soldiers with a large stick. There was also a beautiful princess who floated about the stage singing songs and a man who stood off to one side and every now and then he would bang together a pair of large brass cymbals. I don't remember much else about the show except there were two little monkeys running about the stage who kept running out into the audience and then returning to the stage with morsels of food to eat. I remember this got a very big laugh.

"My father said the woman was a pretty good singer, but not as good as Huang Kuang Sheng, who, according to my father, was the most famous opera singer to ever grace the Island of Hainan. Then the show was over and we stopped at a food peddler. There were all sorts of food peddlers crisscrossing the street in search of customers, especially now that the performance was over. They all were doing a brisk business. My father bought some shrimp and pickled radishes and some peanut cakes and some sugar water and we started for home. We ate and drank while we walked.

"The way I remember that day, Wennan Street was even more crowded on the way back. People on bicycles flew past us. Small boys ran up and down the street with kites trailing behind them and small dogs chasing after the tails of the kites. And the shopkeepers were all waving like mad, trying to get everyone they could to buy their wares before the end of the day arrived. Of course at that point all I wanted to do was go into one of the shops, or stop at one of the vendor stalls, but my father said there wasn't time, we had to go home. But then all of a sudden he changed his mind. Just like that he took my hand and said 'Come my little Lei, I want to show you something.'

"We headed over to a vendor's stall across from a shrine of some sort. The ground of the stall was covered with wicker baskets of all shapes and sizes and colors. The vendor was sitting cross-legged in the center of all of those baskets, as if he were a priest keeping watch. My father motioned to the vendor, who quickly jumped to his feet. The vendor looked about at his baskets for a moment, and then his eyes fell on a very large basket with a brown lid and he became very excited.

"My father spoke to the vendor, who then took off the lid and pulled out a gunny sack. I could see that there was something inside the sack, wriggling, trying to get out.

"'What is it?' I asked my father.

"'It is a python,' my father said.

"And at that moment the vendor pulled the string and opened the gunnysack to show us the snake. I thought for a moment my father was going to buy this python, the first python I had ever seen, for he took a good long look at its glistening skin, and he even remarked that it had a good color. 'Nine dollars Mexican,' the vendor said. (These were the days when a Mexican dollar contained one-half again as much silver as an American silver dollar, so that's why everyone based their prices on Mexican dollars.) But my father just shook his head and said he wasn't interested. Of course the vendor was not yet willing to give up a sale and he tried to bargain with my father. 'Seven dollars,' the vendor said. But my father still said no, and the vendor wasn't willing to go any lower. So we left.

"As we walked away, my father told me that seven dollars Mexican was a very good price for a medium-sized python, but he wasn't interested in buying. He had just wanted me to see a python up close. But then he looked down at me and smiled and said 'Remember my little Lei, if you do not want to buy something, you will always get the best price.' I felt like he was revealing a great secret truth about the way the world worked. And in fact he was."

"So your father was a successful Chinese merchant," said a voice from a chair near the plate glass window.

"Well, he was a merchant," said Ms. Trần. "And he was very successful. But he was not Chinese. You see my father's family originally came from Vietnam in the 1840s. They settled in Hoihow and opened up an import/export business on Zhongshan Road, which in those days was called Dajie Street. Business was difficult at first. They adopted a Chinese name so they could secure trading agreements with merchants in Guangzhou on the Cantonese coast. They also maintained their connections in Vietnam and traded with merchants in both Hanoi and Saigon, but they lost one or two junks a year to piracy, some years as many as four, so their profits were not as large as they might have been. My father said this should not have been a surprise because in those days Hainan Island was known as a haven for pirates."

"You mean actual pirates?" cried the voice from the sofa.

"I do indeed," said Ms. Trần. "But in 1863, the British sent in their navy and eliminated the pirate threat in the South China Sea with their cannons. My family's business began to pick up. Then in 1876, the British named Qiongzhou District a treaty port, and my family's business flourished. Trade with the British was mostly in perishable goods, raw sugar, vegetable oils, cattle, pigs, ducks, even frogs. Trade with their Asian partners concentrated mostly on copra, rattan, hemp, medicinal herbs, and timber. By the time my father took over, we were a wealthy family with a beautiful but small colonial style home in Longhua District, not too far from where my father grew up, which was where my father stayed when he was busy with work, and a second home with a view of a river in Wenchang, the home where I was born."

"So tell us, Ms. Trần," said the voice from the chair near the plate glass window, "why did your family move back to Vietnam?"

"Ah, yes," said Ms. Trần, "why did we leave Hainan Island? Well, the short version of the story is that times change. But I suspect you want a somewhat longer version."

Ms. Trần looked up at Abby, who had just returned from the kitchen.

"Do we have time granddaughter?"

"Yes, *Bà Ngoại*," said Abby. "We have time. We have 15 minutes."

"That will be more than enough," said Ms. Trần.

Abby smiled and squeezed herself into a spot on the sofa. She loved the story of how her grandmother and her family escaped from Hainan when the Japanese invaded the island in 1939. To Abby, the story was part romantic adventure, part spy-thriller, and part cautionary tale.

"I think my father had been planning our escape from Hainan Island for years before we actually left," said Ms. Trần. "Looking back now, it seems as if he had sought out the advice of a fortune teller skilled in the art of Qi Men Dun Jia so that he would understand how to preserve his family's wealth in troubled times. The first sign of trouble occurred shortly after my first trip to see the street performers. As I have already mentioned, in those days the Communists were everywhere. What I did not mention is how violent the Communists had become. They became guerilla warriors and waged war against those in power, meaning the Nationalists, and against those who knew how to make money, meaning people like my father. These guerillas would descend upon a village as quickly as lightning, and if they couldn't persuade the villagers to rise up against their landlords, then they would burn the village and the surrounding fields to the ground. Many villages in the countryside near Wenchang, where we lived, had been abandoned because of these lightning raids. Part of the problem, my father said, was that the government had promised certain tax and land reforms in 1927, but for whatever reason nothing had changed. The Communists became more and more powerful because of the ineptitude of the Nationalist government. By 1929, there was random fighting all over the island."

"Did these guerillas ever attack your house?" asked a young man sitting next to Abby.

"No," said Ms. Trần. "But I think my father believed such an attack was a possibility. Our home in Wenchang was very spacious. There was the main part of the house, which contained an entryway and several sitting rooms jutting off to the sides. The main house overlooked the river. And there were many side buildings connected to the main house by roofed corridors. All of the roofs were pitched quite steeply and were made of red tile. Invariably, whenever there was a big storm, dozens of tiles came crashing to the ground. Always there were workmen repairing the tiles. My bedroom was in one of these side buildings. Also there were two courtyards in the center of the house. The first, which was off the main house, is where we sometimes gathered for meals or to celebrate one thing or another. Ah, the table my mother set was something to see. The food was so sumptuous. Bird's nest soup followed by duck with dressing and black duck eggs and steamed rice. Sometimes there was cuttlefish or abalone or pork. And sides of macaroni. And always there were nuts and candies and steamed cake for dessert."

"Mmmmmm," said several voices all at once.

"What about the second courtyard?" someone inquired.

"Yes," said Ms. Trần. "The second courtyard was towards the back of the property, away from the river, and contained many potted plants and also a small vineyard. There was also a narrow building at the far end of the second courtyard, which is where the servants slept."

"You had servants?", said the young woman sitting next to the young man.

Ms. Trần started chuckling softly.

"Of course, we did," said Ms. Trần. "And they were paid quite well, 15 dollars Mexican a month, plus room and board. Still, with the Communists stirring up trouble like they were, I think my father felt like he had become a target. That's when he started investing his profits in gold and diamonds, though I did not know this at the time."

"So why did he wait until 1939?" said the young man.

"I am not sure," said Ms. Trần. "Perhaps he just wanted to be ready. Perhaps he thought things would get better. Or perhaps the fortune teller had told him he should remain on the island until a specific time. I do not know. What I do know is that things got progressively worse over the next few years. In 1931, a band of Communist guerillas executed a landlord near Nadoa. The fact that they had used a sword to carry out the execution in front of all of the peasants who had been beholden to this landlord, and none of the peasants raised a voice of dissent, this fact alone sent chills up and down the spines of every landlord and merchant on the island. My father took note."

"Ughghh," said the young woman. "How ghastly!"

Several others around the living room were reacting in similar fashion. The man sitting by the plate glass window turned away for a moment and looked out at the waters of the bay glistening in the distance.

"Then in 1933, Hainan was hit by a series of devastating typhoons in May and June, which was taken as a very bad sign, because normally the typhoon season did not begin until later in the summer. The typhoons caused flooding all over the island. Many farmers lost their crops, so there was a shortage of food. Villages that depended upon a single crop, like those villages tucked away in the lush forests of the interior of the island that grew only lychee or jackfruit or wampee or bananas, lost everything. In those villages many people starved to death. Then in 1936, the bottom dropped out of the raw sugar market, which plunged Hainan into a depression. Merchants all over the island began to panic, and many started moving their business endeavors to other ports of call, to Penang or Macao. Still, my father was not ready to leave Hainan just yet. 'A boat cannot always sail with the wind,' he would say later when I asked him about the circumstances of our departure."

"So what happened?" asked the young man sitting next to Abby.

"I'll tell you what happened," said Ms. Trần. "1937 is what happened. In 1937, Japan invaded China. It was an awful time, a turbulent time. Nobody was quite sure what to do. To begin with, our leaders were caught unprepared. Chiang Kai-shek, who had become the ruler of China after General Sun died, had been imprisoned by his own generals in December, 1936. Of course when the Japanese began their invasion, he was released and joined forces with Mao to defend the country. But the writing was already on the wall, this is what my father said. 'Japan has been preparing their conquest of China for years,' my father told me. He said there were many Japanese merchants in Hoihow, merchants who had taken up residence in the city in the 1920s but who were, in truth, Japanese spies. My father was also suspicious of the many Japanese *'fishermen'* who seemed to congregate near the port in Hoihow. He said these fishermen did not talk like fishermen. According to my father, they showed more of an interest in the ships that were arriving or departing, particularly the Chinese ships, but also the British. My father was certain there had been Japanese spies in every major city on the mainland as well, and that these spies had helped to open the door to the Japanese invasion. By the end of 1937, the Japanese occupied the major cities of Northern China, and they even sent a Japanese cruiser cruising past the entrance to the harbor at Hoihow, but the guns along the fortified wall exploded and the Japanese cruiser sped off. Of course that sent many into a panic and there was a mass exodus of people from the coastal cities to the villages in the center of the island. But the Japanese were not yet interested in Hainan Island. They were still battling the Chinese army on the mainland, and they were racking up victory after victory. By the end of 1938, the Japanese occupied all of the major ports along the coast, including Guangzhou. After they took Hankou, Chiang Kai-shek was forced to retreat to Chongqing. It would only be a matter of time at that point before the Japanese would invade Hainan Island. Everyone knew this by January, 1939. My father, however, was one of the few who had seen the trouble coming. 'Coming events cast their shadows,' as the saying goes. So my father was the one of the few who was ready for the arrival of the Japanese. Even so, we barely made it out of Hoihow ahead of the Japanese invasion force."

"Oh my God," said the young woman. "I cannot even imagine what that must have been like!"

Ms. Trần smiled softly and continued.

"Two weeks before the invasion," said Ms. Trần, "my father noticed an unusually large number of Japanese cargo planes flying back and forth over the city of Hoihow. This was the last week of January and the skies were very clear so you could not miss the planes. My father pointed to the sky and said 'little Lei, look at that, the Japanese are coming.' I asked him how he knew this and he told me without any visible emotion that there were too many Japanese planes crisscrossing the skies to be anything other than spy planes taking photographs of the ground. He said the same thing had occurred before the Japanese had invaded the cities on the mainland. Of course I wanted to run away the moment he said that, but he took hold of me and said 'be calm, little Lei, we will be gone before the Japanese arrive.' And so I calmed myself with my father's confidence.

"Later that night, my father asked my mother, my sisters and myself to help prepare for our journey into the future. We were eating a dinner of chili soup and not much else in a small room next to the kitchen. We did not usually eat in this room. It was a room without any windows that used to be a pantry; it was a room where we could eat in peace, without the fear of someone spying on us. So I knew a great change was coming from the moment we sat down to the table."

"After we had finished eating, my father said he had been planning our escape for years, but now he needed our help. He led the four of us to the servants' quarters, which had been empty since the sugar market had imploded. (My father had dismissed all of our servants at that point and had turned their quarters into a workroom or a warehouse of some sort.) We sat down at the only table in the room and my father lit two small brass lanterns and whispered. 'Tonight, we are going to become smugglers.'

"Then he had laughed a great jubilant laugh, which startled all of us, even my mother. I remember how handsome my father looked. He was not a tall man. He stood no more than five-foot-six. He had finely chiseled features and bright white teeth. He seemed like a noble sea captain or a wandering hero from an ancient myth standing there in the golden glowing light of the lanterns."

"I would have been terrified," said the young woman.

"There was no time to be terrified," said Ms. Trần. "My father went over to a series of cupboards along one of the walls and pulled out a dozen or more boxes of various sizes, which he placed on the table. Some of the boxes contained diamonds. Others contained gold coins. Then my father pulled out several suitcases, which he placed next to the boxes. He opened one of the suitcases and pulled out several jackets, female sanitary pads, and belts. 'I need you to sew the diamonds and the gold coins into the lining of these jackets pads and belts. There are maybe thirty jackets in all and roughly a few dozens of pads and a few belts. We are going to smuggle our own wealth out of the country.' So we set to work, me, my mother and my two sisters (Gang and Bao), sewing diamonds and gold coins into the lining of the jackets and inside the lining of the pads. Every night after dinner for the next two weeks we headed to the abandoned servants' quarters and worked on our task. It was very exacting work. Our stitches had to be very small, so that no one would notice the jackets had been altered. As for the pads, back then they were very different from what you use today. We also had to make sure we used sufficient padding so that the diamonds or the coins would not be discovered upon a casual inspection of the material. The cloth had to feel like cloth when touched, when folded, when worn, and it had to sound like cloth when shaken or dropped to the ground. There could be no coins clinking together. We worked every night for two weeks from just after dinner until midnight or even later. And then on February 9, 1939, at about 11 in the evening, my father appeared in the doorway of the abandoned servants' quarters and said we needed to finish what we were doing because the Japanese had arrived."

Ms. Trần paused a moment and looked at her granddaughter, a thoughtful expression on her face, and then she continued. Abby, like all the others, was caught in the spell her grandmother had been weaving.

"I still had two more jackets that I needed to finish," said Ms. Trần. "There was small pile of uncut diamonds on the table and maybe a dozen gold coins. But my father said 'Never mind my little Lei, the Japanese fleet is already anchored in the bay, soon they will be coming ashore, let us go.' Then he scooped up the diamonds and coins and put them in his own pocket. We quickly loaded the jackets, those that we did not put on, into the suitcases, and headed to the back gate. A small black car was waiting for us, a friend of my father's. But as we were getting into the car, my oldest sister, Qiang, who was almost 21, broke away screaming and shaking. She said she could not go with us. Her fiancée lived out on Yanjiang Road. She needed to be with him. And, of course, this was the first any of us except my mother had heard of Qiang's fiancée. My father looked at my mother, and she nodded her head, and then my father stepped towards my sister and they spoke a moment in the shadows. Then he took the diamonds and gold coins from his pocket and put them into a small pouch and gave the pouch to my sister. He also gave her one of the suitcases, the smallest one, which contained four jackets. Then he hugged her and then the rest of us climbed into the car and off we went. It was a very strange night. There were sirens going off all over the city. And there were fireworks as well. Not official fireworks. I think maybe some people had just lost their minds in the chaos. And everywhere there were people trying to get out of the city. The streets were packed with people on foot and on bicycles, many of them shouting. There weren't as many vehicles, a few trucks, a few sedans, all of them blaring their horns. We were all very frightened, except for my father. He said he had arranged for a small junk to take us to Vietnam. We were to meet the boat in a small alcove offshore somewhere west of Lingao. It was normally a two-hour journey by car, my father said, but on a night like this, it would probably take much longer. Then we heard the sound of some very big guns in the distance, followed by the sound of machine guns rattling. My father said there was no cause to be alarmed, the Japanese were simply announcing their arrival. But, from the windows of the car, I could see small fires popping up in the darkness. The Japanese were bombarding Hoihow. Those neighborhoods closest to the harbor, which included the Longhua District, where my father had grown up, those neighborhoods were burning."

"But what happened to your sister?" cried the young woman on the sofa.

Ms. Trần was silent for a moment. Her eyes were glistening. In that moment she looked like she was once again a young girl of 16. Then she shifted in her chair and continued.

"We never saw my sister again," said Ms. Trần. "We did receive one letter some months later. I don't how her letter found its way into our hands, but it did. She must have sent it within the first few weeks of the arrival of the Japanese. She said by daybreak of that first day, the Japanese had sent soldiers and tanks and even some cavalry ashore. It was almost like a festival parade, she had said. She also said that from what she saw, only the native Chinese had died. She saw only empty Japanese stretchers and assumed that that meant not a single Japanese soldier had died during the battle. Of course, she and her fiancée had gone to the compound of the Presbyterian mission in the Qiongzhou District, but there were too many Chinese begging for assistance, so they were turned away. Later, her fiancée was picked up by some Japanese soldiers and taken away. The two of them were trying to make their way back across the city when they had been stopped by a Japanese officer. The officer had asked them where the airfields were, but neither Qiang nor her fiancée knew the answer. They did not know about any airfields. That's what they tried to communicate to the Japanese officer, but he became angry and ordered his men to take Qiang's fiancée away. In her letter, Qiang said she spent several days trying to find out where they had taken him, but no one she spoke to knew anything. She would write, she said, when she had better news. But that was the last letter we received. After the war, my father went back to Hainan Island to try and find her, but she had vanished completely. He was not the same after that. I suppose I wasn't either."

"And what about the rest of your journey," asked the man sitting by the plate glass window.

Ms. Trần looked over at Abby again, this time with an expression of gratitude on her face.

"The rest of our journey was surprisingly uneventful," said Ms. Trần. "We boarded the junk while it was still dark, but we didn't head out to sea until sunrise. Our junk was very small and curved like a banana is curved. Mostly it was a dull brownish-red in color, except near the back, the top portion was painted a dull yellow color. There were also three patchwork sails made of red silk and two eyes painted near the prow, one on either side. It kind of looked like a plucked chicken, I told my father, and he laughed, but his laughter was also filled with tears. 'Why are you crying, father?' I asked. But he said nothing. 'Is it because of the Japanese?' I asked him. And still he said nothing. And then I became very serious and I said, 'Father, tell me, why did the Japanese come to Hoihow? Why did they invade Hainan Island?' And my question seemed to bring him back to himself. He blinked his eyes a moment, as if he were waking up, and then he said 'Because my little Lei, Hainan Island is and always has been the tail of the dragon that is China. And if you control the tail of a dragon, you control the dragon.' Then he smiled at me and made as if he wanted to close his eyes and sleep, but I had one more question. 'Father, tell me one more thing. What are we going to do? Where are we going?' I asked him. 'We are going to Saigon, my little Lei,' he said. 'We are going as far away from China and the invading Japanese as we can. Besides, we have relatives in Saigon.' So that is where we went. We went to Saigon. We would be safe in Saigon because Saigon was in Vietnam and Vietnam was governed by the French and the Japanese were not at war with the French. The journey from Hainan Island to Saigon took two weeks. We had mostly fair weather. Twice a storm came up and we took shelter in an alcove somewhere along the Vietnamese coast, and then we continued our journey south. When we arrived at our destination, my father gave the captain one of our jackets. Little did we know that the Japanese would follow us to Vietnam within a year. By October, 1940 they had assumed control of the country, though they allowed the French colonial government to remain as a puppet regime. By 1941, the streets of Saigon were filled with Japanese soldiers on leave. But that is another story."

Abby and her grandmother were the last two to leave the condo on their way to the wedding. But as they were heading out the door, Abby stopped her grandmother, gave her a big hug, and then she gave her grandmother a thoughtful, probing look, her eyes narrowing slightly, as if she had a score to settle.

"*Bà Ngoai*," Abby said, "I have heard you tell that story a hundred times, and today was the first I ever heard you mention that you had an older sister named Qiang. Why did you never mention her before?"

Ms. Trần was silent for a moment. Then she gave her granddaughter a gentle squeeze.

"I am not sure, granddaughter," she said. "I will have to think about that. But when I have an answer, you will be the first to know."

# Chapter Four
## The Prayed-for Child

**"Oh my, you make such a gorgeous couple," said the photographer as she snapped the first of many pictures of Emily Vuong and David Nguyen on their wedding day.**

Emily and David were standing in front of the entrance to the San Francisco Conservatory of Flowers, a historic landmark that had been the scene of thousands of weddings for generations. The Conservatory was a beautiful example of Victorian architecture and the oldest public wood-and-glass structure in America. It gleamed a brilliant white in the late afternoon September sun.

The happy couple was standing directly in front of the glass windowed atrium, with the stunning glass dome of the Conservatory rising up behind them. The glass of the dome was painted white.

Emily was wearing an elegant white strapless brocaded wedding gown with a band of pearls around her waist. She was also wearing pearl earrings and a pearl neckless to match the gown, and a mesh-net veil made of silk. Her right hand was holding a bouquet of orange, pink and red roses. Her left hand was holding onto David's arm.

David was wearing a traditional black tuxedo with a black and white striped tie and a red rose in the front pocket of his jacket.

"And one more of just the bride and groom," said the photographer. "How about one over by the steps, with the bridge in the background."

David and Emily followed the photographer through the middle of a sea of white folding chairs (five rows of six chairs on either side of an aisle) that had been set up for the wedding ceremony. The ceremony would not begin for another hour, but David and Emily and their wedding party had left Abby's downtown San Francisco condo immediately after the second tea ceremony was over so they could take some pre-wedding pictures. The photographer had said they needed to take advantage of the afternoon light.

"That's perfect," the photographer said as she snapped several more pictures. The happy couple was standing at the top of the steps leading up to the Conservatory. Behind them was a walkway divided down the middle by a bed of red and orange marigolds, and at the end of the walkway was a small Victorian style bridge. The scene was like a fairytale.

Then the photographer took several pictures of Emily with her bridesmaids and then several with David and his groomsmen.

Then David saw his mother and his great-grandmother standing in front of the entrance to the Conservatory. His mother was waving at him, trying to get his attention. David smiled and turned to Emily and whispered in her ear.

"Here we go," he said. "It's your last chance to turn tail and run."

Emily laughed.

"Not on your life," she said.

To the casual observer, the wedding between Emily Vuong and David Nguyen was like any other wedding. But to Arnie Vuong, the father of the bride, it was the culmination of a long journey that had begun with two promises. The first was a promise he and his wife had made to his wife's grandmother one month before their own wedding day. The second was a promise he and his wife had made to each other the day their daughter was born. As Arnie walked his daughter down the aisle, he was thinking about those two promises and how eagerly his wife had been looking forward to the day their daughter would be married. The memory of that journey was very powerful. In fact, it is fair to say that after Arnie returned to his seat, only a part of him was watching his one and only daughter become a part of the Nguyen family. There was another part, a part that he had buried for years, that was now reliving the journey that he and his wife had begun 21 years earlier.

Arnie met the beautiful Vietnamese woman who would be his wife, Lan, on the UCLA campus in 1989. He was just starting medical school and she was a graduate student in the Chemistry program. They met at the Charles E. Young Research Library. He was going in as she was coming out, and then, all of a sudden, they were leaving together. It was a moment when eyes meet eyes and heart encountered heart.

Lan only stood five-foot-one, but in Arnie's imagination she became the sun and the moon and everything in between. Like Arnie, Lan's parents had been killed during the Vietnam War. Lan's grandmother, Ms. Mai, and Lan arrived in the United States in 1974. Three months after they met, Lan invited Arnie to meet her grandmother.

He remembered how nervous he had been. Ms. Mai was a devout Buddhist, and Arnie was not. He had been worried that she would think he was too worldly for her granddaughter. But his fears had been unfounded. He and Lan had taken her grandmother to a small Vietnamese restaurant in downtown San Francisco. He didn't remember the name of the restaurant, but he did remember how full of energy and humor Ms. Mai had been. Lan possessed a similar vitality.

The moment they were seated, Ms. Mai asked them if they were going to get married. When they stumbled over the answer, she laughed and started talking about her own marriage and how she and her husband had been childless for the first two years.

"It was very serious business," Ms. Mai said. "We thought something was wrong, so it was only natural that we sought divine assistance. Of course this was in the days when I was not yet a strict Buddhist. I prayed to the same gods that everyone in our village had prayed to for hundreds of years. So it was not Buddhism exactly. We prayed to the mother goddess Dai Cung Thanh Mau on matters concerning the welfare of mothers. And we prayed to Princess Liễu Hạnh, a heavenly spirit who could help us navigate the spiritual realm. I prayed for a child, of course. I prayed for a daughter since I wanted a daughter. But I could not offer up my prayer until I had first purified my heart and soul. I gave up eating meat and onions and garlic. I took several herbal baths a day. I did this for two months. Then I put on my finest clothes and prepared an offering of fruit and flowers and betel nuts and rice and incense, and I went to the temple in our village. I prayed and prayed. Nine months later my daughter, Lan's mother, was born. I named her Kiều, which means beloved. But we also called her our little Buddha's child, our prayed-for child. She made us very happy."

Six months later, four months before Arnie and Lan were to be married themselves, Ms. Mai passed away in her sleep. It was a peaceful death, and it was not entirely unexpected (Ms. Mai was 97 years old when death came for her). Nevertheless, both Arnie and Lan were heart-broken. They had expected that Ms. Mai would be an integral part of their wedding. She was, they felt, an example of how to live a happy life. Now that she was gone, they wondered what the future would bring.

"How do we make sure that her spirit stays with us," Lan asked.

And Arnie had no answer.

Then one month before their wedding, Ms. Mai came to Lan in a dream. She told her granddaughter that she had hoped to go to the wedding, but now that she was dead, the only way she could attend would be if Lan and Arnie made a prayer offering in her name to Princess Liễu Hạnh. They should make this offering one week before the wedding. Then on the day of their wedding, again invoking Ms. Mai's name, they should pray to the mother goddess Dai Cung Thanh Mau that their marriage would be blessed with a beautiful baby daughter. Finally, in the days after their wedding, to prove that they were worthy of the mother goddess's blessing, they needed to go to a Buddhist temple and make a prayer offering to the mother goddess, the same kind of prayer offering that Ms. Mai had made when she was a young woman hoping to be a mother.

Naturally, Lan and Arnie did just as Ms. Mai had instructed, and within one month of their wedding, Lan was pregnant.

Eight months later, Emily was born.

That is when Lan and Arnie made an additional promise to each other, a promise that became the cornerstone of their happiness. They promised each other that they would both be there to see their daughter, their prayer-child, get married. Yes, they had felt the presence of Ms. Mai at their own wedding. They knew she had been watching over them. But they had been acutely aware of the absence of their family when they got married. Neither Lan's or Arnie's parents had been there. The joy of their wedding day had been tinged with sadness. That is why they promised their infant daughter that they would attend her wedding. They were determined that on that day of days, Emily would know only joy.

So that is what Arnie was thinking as he walked his daughter down the aisle. That is what he was thinking after he had returned to his seat. That is what he was thinking during the entire ceremony. In effect, he was attending both his own wedding and his daughter's at the same time.

Then his daughter and David traded vows and embraced, and Arnie was suddenly returned to the present. He saw the joy on his daughter's face, and though he knew that Emily missed her mother greatly (as he did), he also knew that she was surrounded by the love and joy of family, both her own small family (which included only Arnie and his uncle) and the Nguyen family, her new family, and so her sadness had faded as starlight fades with the coming of the morning sun.

"Do you see our daughter?" Arnie Vuong whispered to the spirit of his wife. "Do you see the joy on her face? We have succeeded, Lan. We have kept our promise."

After the wedding ceremony, of course, was the reception, which was held inside the Orchard Pavilion, a banquet tent adjacent to the Conservatory. The tent (roughly 65 feet by 34 feet) had been elegantly decorated. The decorators had placed a series of paneled silk curtains along the back wall to suggest the opulence of bygone days. The curtains were a soft, pinkish-white hue but were backlit by soft yellow lights placed on the floor, so the color was constantly changing. The interplay of light and color created a dappled effect both on the curtains and on the ceiling of the tent.

The entrance was also hidden by a curtain, which meant that the guests had no idea what to expect until they were inside.

Half of the pavilion was given over to the banquet tables. The long table for the wedding party had been placed along the wall of windows (opposite the back wall). There were also eight round tables placed with geometric precision so that each guest had a view of the bride and groom.

Each table featured a centerpiece of red and yellow orchids. There were also half-a-dozen potted palm trees scattered about. A dozen or more yellow paper lanterns hung from the ceiling. The other half of the pavilion featured a string quartet, which was playing as the guests arrived for dinner. The string quartet played classical music throughout the meal.

Afterwards, the string quartet was replaced by a DJ, who played dance music until 11 p.m..

As the father of the bride, Arnie was seated at the table for family and honored guests. He was sitting between his Uncle Joseph and Abby Nguyen. Abby was sitting next to her husband, Daniel. Across from them sat Ms. Trần (Abby's grandmother), Ms. Kim (Abby's mother), and one of Abby's close friends, Michiko Fukuizumi, who, worked in the financial sector.

Most of the conversation during dinner was about the wedding itself and where David and Emily were going for their honeymoon (Dubai and the Fiji Islands, a gift from the Nguyen family) and how bright the future seemed.

Then Emily and David cut the wedding cake and everyone lifted their glasses for a Champagne toast. And after that, the younger crowd started to dance to the dance music at the other end of the pavilion.

The older crowd, which included Arnie and his uncle, Abby and her husband, Michiko, Ms. Kim, and Ms. Trần, waited for the dessert cart to roll up to their table. The dessert cart had an assortment of French pastries, as well as coffee and hot tea, for those who wanted a little more.

Abby, Daniel, and Michiko each took a single pastry. Arnie and his uncle each took two. Everyone had coffee. And while they were busily eating and drinking, Ms. Trần started talking about her life in Saigon during the Japanese occupation.

"I was 16 years old when we left Hainan Island for Saigon," said Ms. Trần. "It was a dramatic change. It was like stepping from an ancient past, without even the hope of electricity, into a modern world where always there was the glow of an electric light."

Ms. Trần paused a moment and looked at her daughter, Ms. Kim. The two women looked at each other with compassionate eyes.

Then Ms. Trần continued with her story.

"Of course my daughter will tell you I am exaggerating when I say that Hainan Island had no electricity. And she is correct. But the difference between these two places was immense. On Hainan Island, very few people owned automobiles. Most people traveled by wagon or on foot. On Hainan Island we lived on a wealthy estate, but only a few rooms were wired for electric lights. In Saigon we lived in a two-story colonial house in the middle of a colonial city under the control of the French. So of course it was very modern by comparison."

"I cannot even imagine living in the world you describe, Ms. Trần," said Michiko. "It all sounds very exotic to me. What was your house in Saigon like?"

"We lived in a very comfortable house on what the French called La Rue Paul Blanchy."

"I did not call the street where we lived by that name," said Ms. Kim. "I knew our street as Hai Bà Trưng."

"Yes, that is true," said Ms. Trần. "But you did not live in that house until many years later. By then the government had done away with most of the French names in the city. But in 1940, it still had its French name. To me it seemed that we had all of a sudden become a part of the modern world. The electric tramway went right past our house. I could watch it from my bedroom window. My father said he chose this location deliberately. He owned a warehouse near the Da Kao Market, which was north of where we lived and was also on the tram line. And he owned a few more warehouses south of where we lived between Rue Douaumont and Quai de Belgique, so that he had access to a narrow channel which flowed into the Saigon River. My father called this creek the Gia-Dinh channel, but which the French called it arroyo-Chinois. It was a very narrow creek, and because it traversed the middle of a city, the banks on both sides were made of stone. All along the channel there were small flatbed river junks moored to the stone bank on both sides. And up along the bank there were dozens of small shops, drugstores, grocery stores, and warehouses. It was a very busy place. To get there, you would have to take the electric tram to Saigon Station and then get out and walk. I went with my father many times, but never alone. It was always very exciting because there was so much going on. But my father said I should never go down to the Quai de Belgique by myself. And this was especially true after the Japanese took over."

"I hope you do not mind that I am Japanese," said Michiko.

Ms. Trần smiled at Michiko, a warm grandmotherly smile. "No, child, I do not mind," she said. "I have known many good people who were Japanese. Besides, that was many years ago. Your mother was not even a twinkle in the eye of your grandmother. But I do think you should hear what a survivor from the time of the Japanese invasion of Indochina has to say about what happened."

Michiko nodded, a gesture of respect.

The dance floor on the other side of the pavilion had

become very crowded, but for some reason the sounds of the music and of young people laughing seemed very far away. It was as if the wedding has become a dream and the story Ms. Trần was telling was the only reality.

Ms. Trần continued.

"When the Japanese came, life changed once again," said Ms. Trần. "But at first we did not know what was happening. In 1940, the Japanese government was promoting the idea of 'Asia for Asians.' So we did not think the war between China and Japan would expand to include the rest of Indochina. Some people felt that the Japanese might even help us get rid of the French. But my father did not agree. He said the French were providing Chiang Kai-shek and the Chinese with supplies to resist the Japanese advance. As many as a dozen freight trains a day were racing across the Vietnam border on the Hanoi to Kunming railway line. My father said it was only a matter of time before the Japanese invaded Indochina."

"Weren't you frightened?" asked Michiko.

"It sounds quite terrifying," said Arnie Vuong. "Like something out of the pages of a spy-thriller."

"I do not think 'frightened' is the correct word," said Ms. Trần. "My father was a realist, and by this time I was used to bad news. It was just one more thing to prepare for."

"So what did you do?" asked Michiko.

"I do not know all of the politics," said Ms. Trần. "But I do know there was not much we could do. In 1940, the Japanese invaded northern Vietnam. In September 1941, they arrived in Saigon. I remember the day they arrived very vividly. It was like a parade. There was truck after truck filled with Japanese soldiers. The trucks were moving very slowly along Boulevard Gallieni and there were many people lining the street on both sides. Many were cheering, as if the Japanese had liberated our country from the French. But what was very strange was that there was a French gendarme on every street corner. My father later told me that the Japanese were too busy with the war against China, so they let the French stay. The French would run the country and the Japanese would run the French."

"But what was it like with the Japanese?" asked Arnie.

"I am not sure how to answer that," said Ms. Trần. "At first it was not too bad. There was a curfew, of course. But life went on. The Ben Thanh market was as crowded as ever. Bicycles and cabs and taxis and buses filled the streets. But then you began to see Japanese soldiers on leave. They walked about as if they owned the city. Then you began to get reports of soldiers beating young Vietnamese men with clubs. My father said these young men were angry because the Japanese would take whatever they wanted without paying. They had not yet learned to keep their mouths shut. Then you began to get reports that people in the rural parts of Vietnam were starving. because the Japanese were forcing them to grow cotton instead of rice, and much of the rice that was grown went to feed Japanese troops. Then in 1944, all of Vietnam was engulfed in a series of devastating typhoons which flooded the countryside. The rice crop was ruined. In Saigon we were still able to get enough to eat. But in the north, millions died. It was the worst famine in country's history."

"How horrible," said Michiko.

And everyone at the table nodded in agreement.

"Yes," said Ms. Trần. "But the worst was yet to come, at least for me. You see during the time of the famine, the Communists began to raid some of the rice storage facilities so that the people would have enough to eat. Their reputation began to grow. Again, this was happening mostly in the north, but the aftershocks of those raids traveled all the way to Saigon.

"What she means is the reprisals that came afterwards," said Ms. Kim.

"Reprisals?" said Arnie.

"Yes," said Ms. Trần. "You see the efforts of the Communists in the north were supported by people in the south, people in Saigon. After the raids, the French government began to crack down on the Communists, and anyone who might be sympathetic towards their cause."

"But I thought the people in South Vietnam hated the Communists," said Michiko.

"That was much, much later," said Ms. Trần. "In the 1940s, the Communists were viewed as saviors. You see, the French had been exploiting the Vietnamese people for 100 years by that point, and when the Japanese arrived, this exploitation only became more severe. During World War II, many people thought the Communists would help us take back our country. But this did not happen."

Ms. Trần paused for a moment and sipped some of her coffee. Abby smiled at her grandmother and then looked past her to the young people who were still dancing. The music had slowed down, so it was not as crowded as before, but it was still difficult to see who was who. Then she spied her David dancing with his new wife. Their arms were wrapped tightly around each other and they were dancing very slowly. It almost seemed like a photograph. Abby said a short prayer of thanksgiving. Their world and her grandmother's world were light years apart, and Abby was very thankful for this.

"So what did the French do?"

It was Michiko who had asked the question.

"The French all but destroyed the Communists in the north," said Ms. Trần. "Those that were not killed fled to the mountains."

"And in the south?"

"In the south they began arresting collaborators,"

said Ms. Trần. "Hundreds of people were arrested, including my father."

"You mean your father was working with the Communists?", asked Arnie.

"No, no," said Ms. Trần. "My father was just a businessman. But the French thought he might be supplying the Communists with everything from bags of rice to bullets, so they arrested him. He was gone for five days, and then they let him go."

"So what happened to him?" asked Michiko.

"I do not know," said Ms. Trần. "He never spoke about those five days. But afterwards, well, two days after he came home, just as we were finishing dinner, he told us that the French had seized control of two of his three warehouses. My mother and my sister, Bao, began to cry, but my father said there was no need to cry. We were not going to starve. We still had the one warehouse. And then it seemed like my father was talking directly to me, at least he was looking at me with a very measured look on his face as he spoke. 'Some families can lose everything,' he said, 'and yet in a very short while they can rebuild their wealth. Our family is like that. Our family has always been like that.' And he was right. We had lost much of our wealth when we left Hainan Island in 1939. And the war years took the rest. The French took two of our warehouses in 1944, and in February, 1945, we lost the other two warehouses because of an errant Allied bomb. But when the war was over, we once again began rebuilding our wealth, and by 1954, we had regained most if not all of what we had lost."

"How did you do it?" asked Michiko. "How did you rebuild your fortune?"

"That, my dear child," said Ms. Trần, "is a story for another day. But it is getting late, and I am not as young as I used to be. Besides, it is not just my story, it is also my daughter's story, and my granddaughter's story."

Michiko nodded and smiled and then looked over at Abby, who was also smiling. The musicians had finished their last song and the wedding guests were beginning to depart. Abby was helping her grandmother to her feet. Abby's husband and Ms. Kim were heading for the exit. Mr. Vuong was talking with his daughter before she and David left for their hotel. (Their plane to Fiji did not leave until the next morning, so they were staying at the Hyatt Regency in San Francisco.) But Michiko did not get up from her chair just yet. She sat there a while thinking about Ms. Trần's remarkable story.

It was a story of persistence and discipline in the face of incredible adversity. It was a story that anyone interested in how the wealthy make their fortunes would want to hear. She wanted to hear it. She wanted to hear how Ms. Trần rebuilt her fortune in Vietnam between 1945 and 1954. She wanted to hear how Abby's mother, Ms. Kim amassed her own fortune in the years that followed. And Michiko was certain that those budding entrepreneurs who attended her financial workshops every other weekend would want to hear these stories as well. She would talk to Abby in the morning about having Ms. Trần and Ms. Kim speak at one of her workshops. Maybe they could capture the talks on video so that they could share these stories with multiple audiences.

Then Michiko took one last sip from her coffee cup and got up from the table. Already the Conservatory staff was breaking down the tables and stacking the folding chairs on a cart. Michiko hurried to the exit, the last of the wedding guests, and headed to her car. 'Yes,' she thought to herself, 'it is a remarkable story indeed.'

# Chapter Five
## Understanding Your Wealth Scale

**"Good morning Ms. Trần. Good morning Abby," said Michiko. "I am so very happy you are here. Ms. Trần, my students are very much looking forward to hearing you tell your story."**

The three women were standing on the sidewalk in front of a corner storefront at a strip mall located on North Capitol Avenue in San Jose, California. The entire strip mall seemed vaguely Spanish in its design with beige walls and red tile roofs.

It was a bright sunny Saturday morning.

This specific storefront had been designated by the mall management as community space which could be rented by any community organization. The space contained six narrow tables (2 feet by 8 feet) arranged classroom-style in the middle of the room. There were four folding chairs for each table. Along the wall opposite the plate-glass window, there were two additional tables with four computers hooked up to the Internet. Along the wall opposite the corner entrance, there was a white screen and a video console. Behind the white screen, there was a white board. There was also a narrow hallway that lead to a small kitchen, a storeroom, and a bathroom.

Michiko rented the space every Wednesday evening from 7-9 p.m. and every Saturday morning from 10 a.m.

until noon to hold a variety of financial workshops for people from the community. She held workshops on everything from basic financial literacy to planning for the future to preparing tax returns to how to become an entrepreneur. She also talked with her students about various careers they might wish to explore.

"I've been talking to my students for the last month about your upcoming talk," said Michiko. "Not to put any pressure on you, Ms. Trần, but they think you are a financial guru."

Michiko laughed, a soft, cheerful laugh, and pointed to a sign in the plate-glass window that said: "UNDERSTANDING YOUR WEALTH THERMOSTAT: THE KEY TO MAINTAINING YOUR WEALTH IN DIFFICULT TIMES – A TALK BY MS. TR□N LE."

Both Abby and Ms. Trần smiled.

"I brought you a coffee," said Abby.

"From the Starbucks at the other end?", said Michiko.

"Of course," said Abby. "What else."

Abby handed Michiko a grande-sized café latte.

"You read my mind," said Michiko. "I've been here since nine getting things ready and needed a little boost."

Michiko breathed in the aroma of the coffee and then took a sip. Then she opened the door to their home for the next two-and-a-half hours.

"What do you think?" she said.

Michiko had put up a number of large Technicolor poster prints of Vietnam, including several of Saigon.

"Abby, here's where your grandmother will sit during her presentation," Michiko said.

She pointed to a black leather armchair towards the front of the room but to one side of the white screen. There was also a small table next to the table with three bottles of water.

"I created a digital presentation with the photos you

gave me," said Michiko. "I thought we could show the pictures while your grandmother was speaking."

"What a great idea," said Abby.

"I'll operate the video console," said Michiko. "But I did want to go over a few things with you so we're all on the same page."

"Sure," said Abby.

Abby and Michiko moved over to the console and began talking about the presentation. Ms. Trần sat down in the black leather chair. She was listening to every word that passed between Michiko and her granddaughter. But she was also looking at the Technicolor posters of Vietnam.

Then the front door opened and two students hurried through. They were both young men, in their late twenties. They were dressed in khakis and polo shirts and they each carried an iPad.

Michiko waved for them to sit down.

"You are early," she said, smiling.

"We are always early," they said.

They sat down in the front row and turned on their devices so they could take notes.

Abby turned to her grandmother.

"Are you ready *Bà Ngoại*," she said.

"I am ready, granddaughter," said Ms. Trần. "That is in fact the subject of my talk. In our family, all of us were born ready."

Ms. Trần spoke for 90 minutes about her life in Saigon after the end of World War Two. She devoted the first half of her talk to how she and her husband established an import/export company that specialized in trading rice and textiles. During the second half of her talk, she spoke about the birth of her daughter Kim and life in Saigon during the Fifties and how they were able to afford private tutors for Kim. Photographs flashed across the white screen as Ms. Trần talked.

Seventeen students attended the talk. Eleven were of Vietnamese descent and included a family of four (the Hope family). Four were of Mexican descent and three had recently immigrated from China.

"I met my husband, Chen Duy, on September 9, 1945," said Ms. Trần.

"I met him at a rally in what was then called Maurice Long Park," said Ms. Trần. "The rally was in support of Ho Chi Minh, who one week earlier in Hanoi had proclaimed that Vietnam was now free, that we would no longer be under the thumb of other nations."

"Of course the American and British troops who had been stationed in Saigon after the end of the war in support of the French, they did not like this rally. They practically surrounded the park, and we even wondered if they would fire upon us. But they did not fire."

"Later that evening, my father told me to forget about politics," said Ms. Trần. "He said the world would not give Vietnam its freedom, not yet. He told me to focus on business instead. He was right, of course. Two weeks later, thousands of British troops arrived in Saigon to support the French, so the Vietminh attacked."

"There was fighting in the streets of Saigon for several days," said Ms. Trần.

"But the Vietminh were forced to abandon the urban areas of the country, and by Spring of 1946, the French were once again in control of the cities of Vietnam, and Ho Chi Minh and the Communists hid in the mountains and began to conduct a guerilla war against the French."

"And I did what my father advised," said Ms. Trần. "I focused on business."

"What about your husband?" asked one the students.

Ms. Trần nodded politely, a pleased expression on her face.

"My husband, Chen Duy was from Hainan Island," said Ms. Trần, "just as we were. His family had also been merchants. So we had many things in common from the very beginning."

"In 1947, we were married."

"Duy went to work for my father," said Ms. Trần. "My father had built a new warehouse on Quai de l'Argonne, a short walk from the botanical gardens."

"So, at first, Duy began working for my father," said Ms. Trần. "We both wanted to establish our own business, but we could not do this at first. In 1948, our only daughter Kim was born."

"That year was incredibly busy," said Ms. Trần. "I spent most of my time looking after little Kim. But in 1949, with a small loan from my father, we opened a dry goods shop on Rue Catinat."

"Rue Catinat used to be filled with exclusive French shops with the latest fashions from Paris," said Ms. Trần. "But after the end of World War II, many of the French shops and businesses closed their doors and were replaced by Vietnamese businesses. My father said this was because of Ho Chi Minh and the Communists and the guerrilla war they were fighting against the French in those days."

"Was it difficult living in Saigon with a war going on?" asked another student.

"The war against the French did not really affect the way we lived in Saigon," said Ms. Trần. "Our shop on Rue Catinat thrived and we expanded our business. In effect, we became an import/export company. By 1952, we owned four warehouses in Saigon, twice as many as my father, and we owned two more warehouses in Hanoi. We had trade agreements with companies in Thailand and in China, and we were shipping rice and textiles all over Vietnam and beyond."

"That sounds like an incredible rate of growth!"

exclaimed a third student.

"Yes," said Ms. Trần, "we had created a multi-million-dollar company in only three years."

"What was the key to your success?" asked a woman in the front row,

"Our distribution network was one of the keys to our success," said Ms. Trần. "Also, we had a keen sense of what people needed at that time. We were capitalists. We believed in capitalism."

"What about the Communists?" asked a student in the back row. "How did you feel about the Communists, the Vietminh?"

"We supported the Communists," said Ms. Trần, "but only because they wanted to help Vietnam regain her freedom. We did not support Communism in general. Capitalism, the free exchange of goods and services, was the lifeblood of the country. That is why the war between the Communists and the French had no impact on our lives in general."

"But weren't the Vietminh against everything you were trying to accomplish?" asked the voice from the back row.

"No," said Ms. Trần, "they were not. They could have put bombs in the city. They could have blown up the roads. They could have brought our growing economic prosperity to a standstill. But they did not do these things, because that would have been to go against the people of Vietnam."

Ms. Trần took a long drink from a bottle of water.

A few of the students were looking at her with wonder in their eyes. A few were looking at the photo of rice being loaded onto a barge, which was still on the screen. The two students who had arrived before anyone else were busily typing into their iPads.

Abby looked at her grandmother with eyes that seemed to be asking if she was getting tired or if she wanted to continue. Ms. Trần smiled at her granddaughter.

"Now, where were we before we started talking about the Communists?" asked Ms. Trần.

"We were talking about your multi-million-dollar business," said one of the students with an iPad.

"Ah, yes," said Ms. Trần. "By 1952, we had become quite successful. Then in 1953, history repeated itself. The French arrested Duy, just as they had arrested my father during the war years and brought him to the new prison for interrogation."

"The French accused Duy of selling pharmaceuticals, radios, typewriters, paper, weapons, and other contraband supplies for the Communist rebels," said Ms. Trần. "They said he was using our warehouses in Hanoi to bring in these goods over the Chinese border. Hanoi was only four hours from the border. Of course, the French could not prove this. But that did not stop the accusations."

"Was he working with the Communists?" asked the voice from the back row.

"I suppose he was," said Ms. Trần. "Looking back, I am certain he was helping the Communists."

"What happened to him?" asked a woman from the second row.

"He was gone seven days," said Ms. Trần. "They beat him quite severely. He had bruises all over his arms and back and face. And his left arm was broken."

"How horrible," said the woman. "But you survived this just as you survived all of the other ordeals you faced in Saigon."

"Of course we did," said Ms. Trần. "Then in 1954, the war with the French was over. But Vietnam was no longer Vietnam. Now there were two Vietnams, one in the south, which was under the control of the Americans, and one in the north, which was under the control of the

Vietminh and the Chinese."

"We lost the two warehouses in Hanoi."

"We also had to adjust to a new currency system," said Ms. Trần. "Under the French, we had used the piastre, which was equal to 10 French francs."

"But in 1954, the Vietnamese government issued the đồng," said Ms. Trần, "which was only equal to seven French francs. In other words, with the re-evaluation of the currency, we lost 30 percent of our wealth overnight. Once again, any small businesses closed their doors for good."

"How did you overcome such a loss?" asked one of the young men with an iPad.

"Our way of doing business is what saved us," said Ms. Trần. "We still possessed a keen sense of what people needed and wanted. We still understood how to create a viable distribution network. And we now had access to many new products because the Americans had opened the gates to trade with the West. We exported all sorts of Vietnamese goods to the world. And we imported heavy construction equipment and office machines because we did not make these things in Vietnam."

"We were capitalists in an open market economy," said Ms. Trần, "so we did quite well. We were able to hire private tutors for our little Kim."

"In 1956 we hired a yogi who had been trained in India to help us achieve the proper balance between our business goals and our spiritual goals."

"We did everything we could to ensure that our daughter understood that she possessed the knowledge to shape her own future," said Ms. Trần. "We wanted her to understand that no matter what the world might throw at her, she would be able to thrive. She came from a family who believed that acquiring wealth was simply a matter of following a certain set of principles, a certain way of living that rewarded maximum effort. Our family has a very heavy wealth scale. Which means that no matter how many times the world might try to take our wealth away, we will be able to rebuild."

After the presentation, Ms. Trần, Abby, and Michiko joined her students for refreshments and some informal conversation. Many of the students had questions about life in Saigon after World War II had ended or the challenges of running a multi-million-dollar business. Ms. Trần was happy to oblige.

Then, one by one, the students began to leave, and finally, it was only Michiko, Abby, and her grandmother.

"Thank you again, Ms. Trần," said Michiko. "You have given me and my students a great deal to discuss over the next few weeks."

"You are very welcome, Michiko," said Ms. Trần.

"I do have one question for you, however," said Michiko.

"Go right ahead" said Ms. Trần.

"How does one acquire a high wealth thermostat such as your family possesses?"

"The answer is simple," said Ms. Trần, "and it is not so simple. If you want your own children to possess an understanding of wealth and how you can rebuild your fortune no matter how many challenges you face, if you want your children to become masters of their own destiny, then you must begin teaching them when they are very small. You must teach them about wealth and wealth building the same way you teach them their ABCs. Then when they grow up they will be unstoppable."

"I will remember that," said Michiko.

# Chapter Six
## The Law of Attraction

**One week after Abby's grandmother had shared her story with Michiko's students, it was Abby's turn.**

"I'm excited that you have finally decided to share some of your expertise," said Michiko. "What are you going to talk about?"

The two women were standing in line at the Starbucks, waiting to order.

"The Law of Attraction," said Abby.

"Wonderful," said Michiko. "If only everyone understood that what the mind dwells upon, the mind attracts."

"You said it!" exclaimed Abby.

The woman ahead of them turned and smiled at Abby's obvious passion.

"I've been thinking of a café mocha since I woke up this morning," she said, laughing. "And now I'm going to order one! Does that count?"

Abby and Michiko laughed as the woman took her coffee and sat down at the last empty table at the far end of the café. It was quite crowded, even for a Saturday. Even the outside tables were full.

"May I take your order?" asked a beaming, 20-something face.

"I'll have a Caramel Macchiato, grande-sized," said

Abby.

"And your name?"

"My name is Abby."

"I'll have the same," said Michiko. "My name is Michiko."

Abby and Michiko made it to the other side of the strip mall by 9:30. The financial workshop was not scheduled to begin until 10, but there was already a young woman waiting. She smiled demurely when she saw Michiko and Abby approach.

"Hi," she said. "I was beginning to think I had got the time wrong."

"Well, you are a little early," said Michiko. "I hope you weren't waiting too long."

"Maybe 10 minutes," the young woman said.

"You were here last week, weren't you?" asked Abby.

"Yes, I was," said the young woman. "That's why I came back. The story of Ms. Trần was very inspiring. I told my husband about it. I told him that these people, meaning you, could really help us figure a few things out."

"That's very kind of you," said Michiko.

"He couldn't come today," said the young woman. "He had to work. Maybe next week."

"We also offer workshops on Wednesday evenings," said Michiko.

"Really," said the young woman. "Maybe I can get him to come on a Wednesday."

"What is your name?" asked Abby.

"My name is Hope," the young woman said.

Michiko then unlocked the door and the three women went inside. While Michiko turned on the lights and the computers and began to get things ready for the workshop session, Abby and Hope sat down at one of the tables near the front of the of the room and began to talk.

Abby soon forgot all about her coffee.

"My husband works as a machinist for a small machining company out on Oakland Road," Hope said. "They make precision parts, but it's a pretty small shop, so the work is sporadic."

"You mean some weeks your husband doesn't have a job to go to?" asked Abby.

"Try some months," said Hope. "It's been pretty tough going the last year or so. There was a point last year when I was so depressed I didn't know what to do. My husband had been laid off and I couldn't find a job. We didn't have enough money for anything. We lived on canned goods from the Food Bank for weeks."

"Are you working now?", asked Abby.

"I'm trying to," said Hope. "I have a part-time job as a cashier for a 7-Eleven on Santa Clara. But I can only work nights, because during the day I look after my two babies."

"You have two?" asked Abby.

"Two little girls," said Hope. "They're with their grandma-ma this morning, so I could come. But she's getting old. She can't really handle my babies for more than a few hours."

"I see," said Abby. "And what about school?"

"Who has time for school?" said Hope. "And who has the money? It's all we can do just to get by without trying to pay for school."

"Would you go to school if it meant you can build a better life for your family?", asked Abby.

"Well, I guess so," said Hope. "I don't know. What would I go to school for? What if it didn't work?"

"What if I can show you how to make it work?" said Abby. "What if I can show you how to make your dream of a better life come true?"

"You mean you're going to sell me something?"

"No," said Abby. "I'm not going to sell you a thing.

I promise."

"Then what are you going to do?" asked Hope.

"I'm going to tell you the story of how I overcame the same obstacles to a better life that you are struggling with," said Abby.

"That's it?" said Hope. "Just a story."

"It's a pretty powerful story," said Abby.

"You mean like the story Ms. Trần told last week," asked Hope.

"Yes," said Abby. "It's something like that."

Hope nodded, a look of hope spreading across her features, as Abby stood up, coffee in hand, and headed to a small podium that Michiko had set up near the white board. (The white screen was back in the closet in the hallway.)

"Are you ready?" asked Michiko. "Looks like we have a full house this morning."

Abby looked out on the sea of hopeful expectant faces looking her way. There were a dozen or more people sitting at half a dozen tables. In addition to Hope, Abby recognized the two young men from the previous week, the ones who wore khakis and white shirts and shared an iPad. The others were all strangers to her.

For a moment, she felt slightly nervous. She did not often get up in front of people and give speeches. She wondered if her own teachers had felt nervous when they were lecturing. Then she drained the last of her coffee, and feeling suddenly fortified, she began.

"Today I want to talk with you about how to achieve every dream you can imagine," she said. "Today I want to talk with you about 'The Law of Attraction.'"

Abby paused a moment to survey her students.

"Does anyone know what the 'Law of Attraction' is?" she asked.

One of the young men in khakis stirred restlessly, as if perhaps he might offer an answer. But when Abby looked at him, he gave her a sheepish look and shrugged his shoulders.

Abby continued.

"'The Law of Attraction' is the idea that like attracts like," she said. "In other words, if you fill your mind with positive thoughts, then you will attract positive things in your life. If you fill your mind with negative thoughts, then you will attract negative things. Whatever you focus on will come into your life."

One of the students in the back, a heavyset woman in her mid-thirties, raised her hand.

"Are you saying that all you have to do is wish for something and you will get it?", the woman asked.

"No," said Abby. "It's a little more complicated than that. 'The Law of Attraction' demands that you focus on the good things you want for yourself. You try to visualize what they are, what you must do to achieve them, and how to go about staying focused when things get tough,... and they will get tough."

"So it's more of an approach," said one of the young men in khakis. "A philosophy."

"Yes," said Abby. "That's a much better way of looking at it. 'The Law of Attraction' is a way of thinking and living that combines the power of positive thinking with focused action on behalf of those positive thoughts."

"Okay," said the heavyset woman. "That sounds good in theory. But how does it work in principle?"

"You mean what are the rules?" asked Abby.

"Sure," said the heavyset woman. "What are the rules."

Abby headed over the white board, picked up a blue marker and wrote a sentence so everyone could see. She read the sentence as she was writing.

"Rule number one," said Abby. "Every little thought has the potential to grow into a larger thought, and as a thought becomes larger, it grows in power."

Abby turned to the rest of the class.

"What does that mean to you?" she said.

Hope raised her hand and Abby smiled and nodded.

"To me it means you can get caught up in thinking the same thought over and over again," she said. "Like an obsession."

"Good," said Abby. "What else does it mean? What does it suggest to you? Especially that last part about it grows in power?"

"It means that if it grows large enough, it will have the power to impact your life in some way," said the second of the two young men in khakis.

"And is that a good thing?" asked Abby.

"I guess it depends if the original small thought was positive or negative," said the other young man.

An older gentleman sitting at the table directly behind Hope seemed to take courage from the other comments that had been shared and raised his hand.

"What is your name, sir?" asked Abby.

"My name is Leo," said the older man. He looked around at the others in the room and then cleared his throat. "It seems to me that what you are saying is that thinking about something invites that something, whether for good or ill, into your life. So you better be careful about what you are thinking at all times. You better try to eliminate the bad thoughts when they are very small and have little or no power. And you should cultivate the good thoughts."

"Yes, Leo," said Abby. "That's it exactly."

Abby then went back to the white board and wrote down a second sentence.

"Rule number two," said Abby. "You are responsible for creating your own reality."

Abby turned the face her students again.

"So what does rule number two mean to you?" she asked.

"Doesn't it mean the same thing as rule number one?" said the heavyset woman.

"Go a little deeper," said Abby.

"I get it!" said Hope all of a sudden. "It means that if something bad happens to you and your family, or there are bad circumstances in your life, then you have to change the way you think about your life before you can bring about any real change."

"That is very well said, Hope," said Abby.

"But how do you do that?" said the heavyset woman. "How do just change the way you think?"

"That's rule number three," said Abby turning back to the white board. "Listen to the little voice inside you that knows the difference between what is right for your life and what is wrong."

"You mean that little voice we usually ignore?" said the first of the young men in khakis.

Several members of the class started laughing.

"That's the one," said Abby. "But if you listen to that voice, then you can focus your energy on a more positive direction and positive change will happen. What's more, the more you are able to focus on the good things you can achieve, the more quickly that change will take place."

"I like what you're saying," said a fortyish woman. "But what it your life seems to go from bad to worse? How do you stop thinking about all of the bad stuff? I mean there are days when it seems like an endless roller-coaster of bad luck."

"That's rule number four," said Abby. "Focus on the way your life should be, not on the way it is."

"You mean put on a pair of rose-colored glasses?" said the heavyset woman.

"No," said Abby. "This is not about denying the pain and suffering in your life. Instead, it is about refusing to let that pain and suffering sidetrack you from imagining a better future."

"I get what she's saying," said Leo. "She's saying that if you focus on the pain of your life, then you will only attract more pain. But if you focus your thoughts on making things better, a better life, then you will soon begin to live that better life."

"Yes," said Abby. "The process of shifting your thinking is called visualization. You might think of it as a mental trick. Many professional athletes visualize exactly what they are going to do before they go onto the playing field or the court. Visualization helps them center their energies on how to be successful. The same principle applies in every aspect of life. If you want to be successful, you need to be able to imagine that very success."

"Okay," said the heavyset woman. "Suppose I give this a try. You also said that things were going to get tough at some point. So I gather it doesn't always work?"

"No," said Abby. "It always works. It just doesn't always work on the timetable you have in mind."

"So how do I handle those times when I am struggling with disappointment because nothing is working at first?" asked the heavyset woman.

"You keep applying rules one through four," said Abby. "But you have to increase your commitment."

"And how do I do that?'

"Rule number five," said Abby. "I call it the five-minute rule. Take time every single day to focus on the change you want to see. Think about what you must do to make your dreams a reality, visualize your success, and then plan for it. You have to touch your dream every single day. Even if you only have five minutes to devote to changing your life."

"Is there anything else I can do?" asked the woman. "I mean on a practical level."

"Yes," said Abby as she turned back to the white

board. "Rule number six. Avoid negative thoughts and images from any source. That includes television shows and movies that present a negative picture of the world. Remember, when you focus your attention on negative things, no matter where those negative things or experiences come from, you are drawing them closer to you and your life."

"Is there anything else that might help understand how to apply 'The Law of Attraction'?" asked Hope.

"What is true for negative experiences is also true for the negative people in our lives," said Abby. "If you are having bad experiences with the people in your life, you need to begin by imagining how your relationships should be."

"That is easier said than done," said the woman.

"Yes, it is," said Abby. "But everything I am sharing with you is easier said than done. All of it requires intense focus and a commitment to never give up."

"Did you apply 'The Law of Attraction' in your own life?" asked the second of the two young men in khakis.

"Yes, I did," said Abby. "My family came to this country in 1975 when I was only six years old. We came as refugees, having lost everything as a result of the Vietnam War, so we settled where many Vietnam refugees settled, in the Tenderloin area of San Francisco. My mother worked in a nail salon for a few years and then she opened her own salon. My father worked in a restaurant as a waiter. We were very poor. But we did not stay poor for long."

"Because you applied 'The Law of Attraction'?" asked the heavyset woman.

"Well, I didn't know there was a name for it. It was my mom and dad who learned it when they were in Vietnam at a young age," said Abby. "I only learned later, after reading books, that what we were doing in those days was exactly what 'The Law of Attraction' says you should do if you want a better life."

"So you discovered the law on your own!" exclaimed Leo.

Abby chuckled.

"I would love to take all the credit, but no. I had good mentors, my mom, my dad, and many others," said Abby.

She then walked to her manila folder, looking for something. A short time later, she pulled out a picture of a little dwarf sitting on the shoulder of a large person who was about four or five times bigger than the dwarf. She then excitedly passed it around the classroom and continued.

"As you all can see from the picture, a dwarf is standing on the shoulders of a giant. This expresses the meaning of "discovering truth by building on previous discoveries." This concept has been traced to the 12th Century, attributed to Bernard of Chartres. In the English-speaking world, Isaac Newton in 1675 made the metaphor well known until modern time today, as in "If I have seen further, it is by standing on the shoulders of giants."

The classroom suddenly stood still, the piece of paper with the picture on it ended up in Hope's hand, and she forgot to pass it on to the next person after reviewing it. Abby could hear the eerie sound of a fly in front of her. All of the sudden, the attendees, as though they had just heard something that they had never heard before, became entrenched in their own thoughts.

Hope raised her hand, signaling she had a question. Abby nodded in her direction.

"I have never heard of this before in my life. Is there really any proof that all of this actually took place? I mean I'm surprised that this kind of observation actually came about as early as the 12th Century and yet I don't know it"

"Good question, Hope. I'm glad you asked," Abby smiled clearly, relieved at not having to answer what she thought would be a harder question.

"If you have an opportunity to visit Chartres Cathedral in Chartres, France, which by the way was mostly constructed between 1194 and 1220, about 50 miles southwest of Paris, in the stained glass of the south transept of this cathedral is the depiction of the metaphor."

"Amazing!" said Leo.

"At any rate, it began with my mother," said Abby. "She came home one day from the nail salon where she had been working at and she said she was going to open her own business. We did not even question her on this. She spoke with great conviction. She later told me that she could see her nail salon in her mind's eye as clear as day. And then she got down to the work of making what she saw in her mind a reality. She took English language classes. She took business classes. Even though she knew how to run a business in Vietnam, she felt she needed to learn the American system, the American way. She saved her money so she could one day secure a lease for her salon. Three years later, she was open for business. Three years after that, she had three salons in San Francisco. By the time I graduated from high school, her nail salon enterprise was worth well over a million dollars."

"So you learned how to be successful from watching your mom?, said the woman.

"Yes, that is exactly what I did," said Abby.

"What path did you take?" asked Hope.

"After I graduated from high school, I went to the City College of San Francisco for two years," said Abby. "But I knew that was only the beginning. "I wanted to help my mother grow her business, so I went to the University of San Francisco and earned a degree in economics. Then I earned my masters in 1994."

"How did your education allow you to help your mother?" asked the woman.

"My mother did exceptionally well based on her business instincts," said Abby. "Our family has always had exceptional business instincts. But with my education, I saw that we could leverage her assets and grow the business even further. The first step was to turn her nail salon business into a franchise opportunity for others, which we did. We now have over a dozen franchisees and the number is growing."

"Does that mean your mother's company is worth more now than when you graduated from high school?", asked Leo.

"Yes, it does," said Abby. "We quadrupled the value of the company in a little over 10 years. But I didn't want to settle for being well-off, or even rich. I wanted to be wealthy."

"What's the difference between being rich and being wealthy?" asked Hope.

"Being rich means you, as an individual, have a lot of money," said Abby. "Being wealthy means your entire family has a lot of money."

"Wealth is something you pass on to your children and their children and so on?" said Leo.

"Yes," said Abby. "And that's what I wanted to do. I wanted to build an empire to make sure that my children and their children and grandchildren would always have money to be able to do whatever they needed or wanted to do."

"And are you wealthy?" asked the heavyset woman.

"Not yet," said Abby. "But I am on my way there."

"Well that's further than me," the heavyset woman replied.

"That's further than any of the rest of us," said Leo.

"But not if you begin planning now," said Abby. "And take seriously what I've shared with you about 'The

Law of Attraction.' If you imagine it, you can do it."

Everyone in the room broke into a round of applause.

Abby felt a tad bit embarrassed, but she was beaming.

"Are you coming back next week, Abby?" asked the first young man in khakis.

"Do you want me to?" asked Abby.

There was a chorus of yeses and a lot of head nodding.

"How about I bring my mother along?" said Abby. "Then she can tell you her story, which is, in fact, the beginning of my story. Then you can learn from her the way I did."

And with that, the session was over and, one by one, Michiko's students gathered up their belongings and began to head outside.

Twenty minutes later the community room on the corner of the strip mall was empty except for Michiko, who was cleaning up, and Abby, and Hope, who were discussing how Hope might make a better life for herself by tapping into the positive energy of 'The Law of Attraction'.

"So you see," said Abby, "the City College of San Francisco allows you to take classes on a part-time basis, but I think, if you push, you can finish in three years."

"And then I can transfer to the University of San Francisco," said Hope, "just like you did."

"And once you have your degree, the sky's the limit," said Abby.

"Oh, Abby," said Hope. "I'm so excited. I don't know how to thank you."

"Just promise me that if you need any help at all, you will give me a call," said Abby. "Promise?"

"I promise," said Hope.

# Chapter Seven
## The Journey from Vietnam to America

**Abby's mother. Ms. Kim, did not look nearly as comfortable as Abby had standing up in front of Michiko's students.**

"I don't know if I can do this," she had told Abby as they were walking into the classroom with Michiko the following Saturday morning.

"Of course you can do it, mother," Abby had said. "You are a natural, just like grandmother."

"You will help me out if I get stuck," Ms. Kim had asked.

"Yes, mother," Abby had said. "But you won't get stuck. You will be a little nervous at the beginning. I was nervous at the beginning when I got up in front of the students last week. But as soon as you begin, the nervousness will disappear."

"I hope so," Ms. Kim had said.

"You will be fine," Abby had countered.

And then Ms. Kim began her talk. The same dozen students that had filled the classroom the previous week were back. In addition, the woman had brought a friend, an older gentleman, very thin, white hair, a white beard, neatly trimmed; and Hope had brought her husband. ("The kids are with their grandma again," she had said to Abby as they sat down.)

"When I was a little girl, we lived in a small two-story house not too far from my parent's dry goods shop on Rue Catinat. As I recall it was beige in color, or a pale yellow. I remember it was on a very busy street with lots of traffic."

Ms. Kim paused a moment and looked over at Abby, who only nodded her head slightly, a motion that said everything is OK, keep going.

"I do not remember those days as difficult days," said Ms. Kim. "though there were many who said the days after the war were difficult indeed. It was very busy, but not difficult. During the week, a tutor came to the house to instruct me in various academic subjects. On Tuesday and Thursday afternoons, a yogi came to the house to instruct me on how to approach life. Her name was Ms. Manisha, and she taught me how to free my mind and stay positive about my future. I remember she was very old. She wore a white robe and sandals, and she had long gray hair which was pulled together in a single braid. After my lessons, she would sit with us at the long dining room table and we would eat an early supper. Looking back now, I realize that Ms. Manisha was teaching me what my daughter knows as 'The Law of Attraction'. She helped me to understand that true success in life, true happiness, was the result of constantly examining your thoughts, sifting through the bad from the good. I learned from her how to purify my thinking and visualize the world as it should be. She taught me that the longer I focused on this ideal world, the more likely I could call that world into being. If Ms. Manisha had not taught me these things, I do not think I would survived the terrible ordeal on Bidong Island."

"Was it easy for you to free your mind and learn stay positive?" asked Hope

"I wouldn't say it was easy, but Ms. Manisha was a genius. She was able to break it down into steps so that even a 10-year-old can do it," Ms Kim shared.

"So, would you be able to share that with us?", Hope didn't give up. She felt something big was coming, so she just had to ask.

"Of course, we can do this after class, as I wasn't prepared for this. Is that OK?" replied Ms. Kim

"That'd be so fantastic," Hope replied with a gleam of hope in her eyes.

Another hand went up.

"What was Bidong Island?" asked Leo.

"Bidong Island is where refugees of the Vietnam War went to escape the Communists," said Ms. Kim.

"So this was after the war had ended?" asked one of the young men in khakis.

"Yes," said Ms. Kim. "It was a terrible time for my family."

"What happened?" asked Hope.

"The war ended in 1975," said Ms. Kim.

Ms. Kim paused a moment to collect herself. It was clear to everyone in the classroom that she was experiencing emotions she had long ago buried. She took a sip of water to steady herself and continued.

"Everywhere in Saigon people started to panic," she said. "Many who had worked for the Americans and the prior government's military were taken away and shot or put in a re-education camp.

Ms. Kim looked steadily at the students in the classroom. She did not say a word for maybe 20 seconds, though it felt much longer. Then she gave a slight nod and said, "That was only the beginning of the dark days that lay ahead."

"What happened next?" said the woman.

"The era of boat people, especially those of Chinese descent is what happened," said Ms. Kim.

"You mean the wave of boat people from Vietnam started because it was part of a plan for the Vietnamese communists to get rid of ethnic Chinese Vietnamese?" said the older gentleman with the white beard.

"No one knows for sure but through the grapevine I heard, yes," said Ms. Kim. "You see, after the war, the Vietnamese government took a hard line against the "Hoa" people, all ethnic Chinese Vietnamese whose ancestors had immigrated from China to Vietnam many years ago to settle and build a new life here."

"But I thought the Vietnamese and the Chinese were allies?" said the heavyset woman.

"Yes and no," said Ms. Kim. "The Vietnamese government was tired of having China dictate how they should behave. They were especially annoyed at the fact that many of the most successful businessmen in Saigon, which was now called Ho Chi Minh City, were either Chinese nationals or were descended from Chinese parents. And what was true in the south was also true all over Vietnam."

"So what did the government do?", asked Leo.

"At first they tried currency reform," said Ms. Kim. "But that didn't seem to have any impact on the Chinese businessmen. They were still in control of the markets, even the black market. Then in 1978, the government declared that they were going to give all of the "Hoa" traders in the country, but especially in the south, an opportunity to leave Vietnam voluntarily. But now, all of their businesses were going to come under control of the government."

"That sounds like an impossible undertaking by any government," said the man with the white beard.

"Well, it happened in Vietnam and if I may remind you, it also did happen to Japanese Americans during World War II," said Ms. Kim. "Many small businesses were raided and their inventories confiscated. And then the government forced thousands and thousands of Chinese Vietnamese to relocate to what they called New

Economic Zones."

Ms. Kim took another sip of water and looked at her daughter a moment with deeply sad eyes. Then she continued with her story.

"It was only a logical next step that the government begin deporting the Chinese Vietnamese in 1978," said Ms. Kim. "Oh, they didn't say they were deporting them. They called them refugees. And truthfully, by then most of those of Chinese descent wanted nothing to do with Vietnam."

"And that's where Bidong Island enters the story?" said Leo.

"Yes," said Ms. Kim. "From 1975 to 1978, Bidong Island was where boat refugees from the war were forced to live while en route to a country that would accept them. But in 1978, the Malaysian government made Bidong Island an official refugee camp. The island was home to thousands. Thousands more left the shores of Vietnam in any kind of boat that would carry them away. Most of these junks looked as if they would sink if a storm came along, and in fact many died at sea."

"How did you and your family escape?"

"My family at that moment was only my mother, myself, and my daughter Abby," said Ms. Kim. "We paid the equivalent of 10 taels of gold per person and boarded a junk on the Saigon River."

"How much is 10 taels of gold?" asked the second young man in khakis.

"Ten taels is, was, about 12 ounces," said Ms. Kim. "We were paying about two thousand U.S. dollars per person to get on that junk to Bidong Island. It was a pretty standard price. I mean, everyone paid. If you didn't pay, you didn't get on the boat."

"And the Vietnamese government was okay with this?" asked Leo.

"I don't know, but again I have heard through the

grapevine that the Vietnamese government was behind it," said Ms. Kim.

"What happened when you arrived on the island?", asked the woman.

"It took us 10 days to even get to Bidong Island," said Ms. Kim. "It is a long journey, over 700 kilometers. On three separate occasions, our boat was boarded by pirates traveling the South China Sea. How we managed to hang onto the few valuables in our possession was a miracle by any definition. Some of those traveling with us were not so lucky. One poor man was roughed up so badly by a toothless thug that he died soon afterwards. My mother said he died of internal bleeding, though how she knew this I could not say."

"How did you survive that ordeal?" asked the heavyset woman.

"My Hope in God and in the goodness of the world kept us from harm," said Ms. Kim. "It was everything my yogi, Ms. Manisha, had taught me. I imagined that we were going to a better world. I saw this world in my mind's eye. That is why when the pirates boarded our junk, they left us alone. I was not focused on pirates. I was focused on a better world."

"How long were you on Bidong Island?" asked the woman.

"We were there almost two years," said Ms. Kim.

"And all that time, you continued to focus on how your lives were going to get better?" asked the white-haired man.

"I did," said Ms. Kim. "It was a very difficult time, but I did not lose my hope in what I had been taught. We lived in a hut made from plastic sheets draped over logs with a piece of corrugated tin for a roof. We paid $10 for a teaspoon of salt or a cup of rice. The latrines were always overflowing, especially after it rained. We were given one gallon of drinking water per day per person."

"It sounds horrible," said the heavyset woman.

"It's amazing that you kept your hope," said the women with too much rogue.

"It's more than amazing," said Hope. "It's inspiring."

"So how did you eventually escape from Bidong Island and come to America?" asked Leo.

"This is the most amazing part of our story," said Ms. Kim. "It is where everything my family has been doing since the early part of the 20th Century begins to converge."

"Oh, I just got goosebumps," said Hope.

"You see, back in 1930, my grandfather had set up an investment account with an investment banker in Hong Kong. Initially, the investments were in rubber, but after Japan invaded China in 1937, my grandfather apparently asked his banker to begin shifting the investments into overseas markets, particularly the London and the New York Exchanges."

"So you were rich and you didn't know it?" said the first young man in khakis.

"No," said Ms. Kim. "We were not rich."

"What happened to the investments?" asked Leo.

"Apparently, whoever took over my grandfather's account in the 1950s was a crook," said Ms. Kim. "He had swindled dozens of clients who had "disappeared" during the war years. Each account had just enough in it to keep the account 'open.'"

"So how do you know all of this?" asked the white-haired man.

"I know because in 1976, the crooked investment banker was arrested on charges of fraud," said Ms. Kim. "The authorities in Hong Kong began to track down the families who had been defrauded. In some instances, it took a few years. The man who was trying to locate us said he had almost given up. He had already been to

Bidong Island twice because he had suspected we were there, based on our ancestry and our Chinese connections. But on any given day, there were as many as 40,000 registered refugees, so going through the lists of names was a hit or miss proposition. But in May of 1980, he decided to give it one more try, and he finally found us."

Ms. Kim smiled a broad smile.

"Once again, my hope in a better world was rewarded," said Ms. Kim. "There was only 10,000 U. S. dollars in my grandfather's investment account, but it was enough to help us get to America. We were given a high priority status and, in August of 1980, we were offered resettlement in America. Our sponsor was a church in Eden Prairie, Minnesota."

"I thought you resettled in San Francisco?" said the second young man in khakis.

"We did," said Ms. Kim. "Our sponsor was in Minnesota, but that did not mean we had to move to Minnesota."

"And it's a good thing you didn't," said Leo. "It would have been quite a dramatic change coming from the tropics. It gets quite cold in Minnesota."

A few of the students started laughing.

"When did you finally arrive in America?" asked the woman.

"We arrived near the end of September, 1980," said Ms. Kim. "We had endured war, poverty, pirates, and an arduous journey across a turbulent sea in a boat that seemed like it would sink at any moment. But there was nothing that could keep us from our destiny."

"Because you believed in your destiny," said Leo.

"Yes," said Ms. Kim. "It is all because we believed, we had hope, and we never stopped believing or stopped having hope."

# Chapter Eight
## A Honeymoon in Fiji

**The honeymoon in Fiji, a wedding gift from his grandmother, was everything that David Nguyen and his new wife, Emily, thought it was going to be.**

"You mean we're really going to Fiji," Emily said.

"Yes," he replied. "We'll be in Dubai and Fiji for a total of 11days."

"Your grandmother is incredible," Emily said.

And David agreed.

They flew from San Francisco and spent four days days seeing the sights of Dubai. They then visited the Sri Subramaniya Swami, the largest Hindu temple in the Southern Hemisphere. David was struck by the vivid, vibrant, rainbow of colors of the temple architecture. Emily marveled at the sense of stillness that seemed to permeate every inch of the temple grounds.

They visited The Garden of the Sleeping Giant and spent the better part of an afternoon wandering through a vast labyrinth of walkways among the orchids and lush vegetation of a tropical rainforest.

Then they boarded a smaller island-hopping plane for the island of Taveuni, which was where their resort was located.

The resort was named the Taveuni Island Resort and Spa, and the moment they checked in, it was a fantasy dream come true.

They had spent the last 7 days in one of the luxury ocean villas, exceedingly spacious accommodations. Their villa was made from native timber and featured floor-to-ceiling windows in every room. The view from their bedroom offered a spectacular view of the heavenly blue ocean.

They spent their days swimming in the lukewarm waters, taking hikes in the rainforest, marveling at waterfalls that plunged hundreds of feet.

They went snorkeling at Rainbow Reef.

They took long walks along the beach, hand in hand, talking about their bright future.

Emily relaxed in the spa while David swam in the pool.

Some nights they ate dinner in the resort restaurant, and what an amazing feast that was each and every time. The last time, on Saturday night, they started off with Rourou soup with fresh bread rolls, followed by seared tuna with salsa verde, and then chocolate silk for dessert.

Other nights, they cooked small romantic meals in their villa.

'Yes,' thought David, 'This honeymoon was everything Emily and I had hoped it would be.'

It was after midnight and Emily was sleeping peacefully. David was sitting at the foot of the bed. He was strangely alert. He sat there a while listening to Emily breathe, and then he got up and walked over to the open window to look out at the shimmering darkness that was the sea. He could see starlight reflect in the waves. He could hear the steady lapping sound made by the waves as they rolled up the beach. It was a comforting sound like the sound inside his mother's womb when he was a little fetus.

David was suddenly overwhelmed by an immense sense of gratitude. Yes, this honeymoon was everything they had thought it would be, but it was only possible because of the generosity of his grandmother, Ms. Kim. Then David realized that his gratitude was not just for his grandmother. He was grateful for the sacrifices that his entire family had made over the years, sacrifices that had made it possible for him to enjoy his honeymoon with Emily in this veritable paradise. He was grateful for his great-great-grandfather's business acumen and his foresight in moving the family from Hainan Island to Vietnam when the Japanese invaded. He was grateful for his great-grandmother's dedication and perseverance during the family's years in Saigon both during World War II and immediately after. He was grateful for his grandmother's ability to think positively at all times. No matter how desperate the circumstances, she had always managed to focus on the good that was to come. And he was grateful for his mother, for her ability to have clarity in all matters...in matters of business, in matters of education, in matters of the family, and in matters of the heart.

Now, he felt it was his obligation to imagine a better life for himself and his Emily. Now, it was his turn to lead the way into a better future.

David sensed someone was looking in his direction. He turned from the window to see a sleepy Emily half-sitting up in bed, squinting.

"Are you coming to bed, David?" she asked.

"Yes, my love," he said. "I'm coming to bed."

"We have a busy day tomorrow."

"Yes," he replied. "And for many more tomorrows after that."

# About the Author

Suzanna is a tax CPA. She began her tax advisory career in 1997 with Arthur Andersen in San Francisco following earning her Master's Degree in Taxation and Bachelor's Degree in Accountancy from San Francisco State University. After twelve years working her way up to a Senior Manager position at Arthur Andersen, Pricewaterhouse Coopers, and Deloitte, advising Fortune 500 companies as well as high technology start-ups, she decided that entrepreneurship was the only way for her to reach her dreams of becoming financially independent. Her entrepreneurship journey started in the real estate area in 2009 and continues to bring her places, meeting new and interesting individuals who are also great friends and mentors.

Suzanna and her spouse of 20 years, Tien, live in Fremont, California with their three children, Lan-Chi, Anh-Khoi and Thai-Dan. She believes in two things: 1) Everyone should know about financial knowledge; and 2) Everyone deserves an opportunity to change their family tree.

*Millionaire Baby: Cracking the Wealth Code - A Double Kaching Wedding* is the third book in the *Millionaire Baby* series.

Made in the USA
Monee, IL
05 November 2026

67375696R00059